If You've Got it to Do....

by Wilma Williams

Copyright © 1996 by Wilma Williams

All rights reserved. No part of this book may be reproduced or transmitted in any form or by any means, electronic or mechanical, including photocopying, recording or by any information storage and retrieval system, without written persmission of the author.

ISBN 0-9621543-8-5

Wizard Works
P.O. Box 1125
Homer, AK 99603

If You've Got it to Do....

Acknowledgements

I would like to express appreciation to the Homer Writers Group for seeing me through my early feeble efforts at writing, and also to Jan O'Meara for her patience, perseverance and assistance with the editing.

Dedication

This book is dedicated to three people who have made my journey through life much more pleasant than it could ever have been without their humor, support and affection.

To my cousin Merlie, even if she did laugh at me when I went bouncing across the irrigation ditches in the goat cart. She has always been there for me in the good times and the bad. We ate our mud pies together up in the Okanogan Valley, rode horseback over the Oregon hills together, and learned together to sew a fine seam to make her mother happy.

To my sister, Loma, whose consideration and affection is always there.

To my friend Lil Miller. I have never spent a minute in her company that was not a pleasure. I never call her that I don't end up feeling better for having talked to her. The closest thing we ever had to an argument was a difference of opinion over the theory of evolution. I think we decided there was nothing we could to about it one way or the other and let it go at that.

Prologue

New Beginnings

Nita braced herself in the bunk, holding her screaming child tightly. Fear clutched her heart as the 70 foot passenger-cargo boat, *Princess Pat*, dove again into the foaming gray waters of Cook Inlet.

Was this the dream she and her husband, Tom, had scrimped and saved to make happen? She thought of her mother and father on the farm in Oregon. Tears welled in her blue eyes. Would she ever see them again?

The wall became the floor. The rolling motion nauseated her. When the boat surged upward she felt like she was glued to the painted surface that had been the wall, while the light bulb's eerie glow radiated from the center of the wall. In this distorted world the odor of diesel and sour vomit seemed to be everywhere.

Her baby cried pathetically. Nita worried that the child might be seriously ill. In spite of the two weeks the family had spent in Anchorage, it might still be the formaldehyde in the milk served on the steamer *Northwestern* aggravating the baby's tender tummy. When Nita had complained to the waiter of the strange odor of the milk he told her the formaldehyde was to keep the milk from spoiling. She had grave misgivings about such drastic measures of preservation.

The month of travel had taken its toll, leaving dark shadows beneath Nita's forget-me-not blue eyes. Her waist-length golden brown hair was in a state of disarray instead of the usual neatly pinned twist at the nape of her neck that was so in fashion.

Nita really feared that their whole little family might perish only a few hours short of their final destination. The boat slowly righted itself as though it had tired of tormenting these helpless humans held firmly in its grip. With this motion the baby loosened her grip on her mother and looked about, catching her breath in ragged little gasps.

"For an eight-month-old girl child you are very noisy," Nita said, smiling weakly at her little daughter.

Nita leaned over and felt for the suitcase beneath the bunk. She found a dry dress. Her last trip out on the deck had left her drenched from the icy salt spray but she had been too sick to care.

Suddenly the door flew open. Her husband, Tom, was there shaking the salt spray from his curly brown hair. She was glad to see him but couldn't help being a bit irritated at the obvious pleasure he was deriving from the trip while she suffered with each new wave. It just wasn't fair.

He smiled at his wife and gave her a quick hug. The baby held up her hands to her father and he picked her up. "Only an hour and a half until we will be inside Kachemak Bay. The skipper says it won't be as rough once we are inside."

"It can't happen too soon," Nita replied, trying to smooth the suitcase wrinkles out of her dry dress. She picked the wire hairpins out of the bunk and attempted to pin up her hair, hating to have Tom see her like this.

"I just want to feel good dry land under my feet again," she said.

In this last month Tom and Nita Shelford, with their baby daughter, Wilma, had traveled from the little western Washington town of Ryderwood to Seattle by train. In Seattle they boarded the *Northwestern* for their northbound journey to Seward, Alaska.

Nita had commented when they boarded the train in Seward, "Tom, this railroad is only two years old. Do you think it is safe?" He felt it was and the very new Alaska Railroad carried the family to Anchorage. It was two weeks before they could secure passage to their final destination of Seldovia on the *Princess Pat*.

True to the skipper's prediction, the waters calmed as they came into Kachemak Bay and then Seldovia Bay. This was the end of their journey. Here they would start their new life in the Territory of Alaska. They looked toward the shore eagerly. Nita held baby Wilma up to see the first glimpse of her new home. Tom came to stand by his wife. She smiled at him.

It was March of 1926 when these things took place. In spite of challenging hazards and discomforts the family survived. I was that baby and the following are tales of my life in the far north.

Chapter 1

With This Ring

The women on my mother's side of the family were solid pioneer women who set great store by family ties. Going back as far as the 1700s my grandmothers boarded the ship, or climbed up on the wagon seat beside their husbands and traveled ever westward until, by the time my mother was born, they had progressed to the Oregon shores of the Pacific Ocean.

Nita was born in little cabin built by her father on the banks of Indian Creek a few miles out of Mapleton, Oregon. When they left their home on Indian Creek in 1906 she was a year old. Uncle Bill, who was 11, carried her on his back as they made their way down the rugged trail.

By 1907 the family purchased 60 acres five miles out of the little farming community of Dallas, Oregon, fourteen miles south of the capital city of Salem.

After graduation my mother went to San Francisco and spent a year in the Salvation Army. Later, with a girlfriend from Dallas, she again left home to see the world. Their limited funds took them as far as southern Oregon before it was necessary to go to work. The small cafe where they found work fed the local logging crew. It was there she met Tom Shelford.

As she filled his coffee cup and served his meals, Nita listened to the stories Tom told of the Welsh coal-mining town of Albia, Iowa, where he had been born to first-generation immigrants. His mother had been born in Wales and his father in England.

It had seemed for a time he would follow family tradition when he went to work in the coal mines at the tender age of 11. For my father it was a negatively memorable experience. He hated every dark, dank day he spent in the mines, living for the day he would emerge into the sun and pursue a different career.

At 16, Tom got a job on the railroad, neglecting to tell them his age. The new job involved shoveling coal, which he had already had five hard years experience doing. This was different from the work in the mines. He was firing boiler on the train, watching the world fly by the window and loving every mile it took him away from those Iowa coal mines. All went well until the railroad people found out their fireman was 16 years old. In spite of his good record, they were forced to let him go. In parting, they gave him a lifetime pass on the railroad and told him to come back when he was 18.

He was devastated, but using that pass he continued his escape by traveling to Montana. On the westbound train Tom got acquainted with his seat mate, a strip-mine owner, and before arriving at their destination was hired to drive team at his mine. When the cold winter weather caused the job to close down, he went farther north, ending up in the Peace River country and filing on a homestead on the river's bank. His love affair with the great outdoors started there, and he thought he would never leave that beautiful Canadian wilderness. However, when he discovered he would have to become a Canadian citizen to receive final papers on his homestead he had to make a serious decision. He loved Canada but could not bring himself to give up his U.S. citizenship.

With that decision, Tom sold his cattle and cabin and went south, riding the train to the southern part of Oregon. Using his boiler-firing knowledge, he got a job firing donkey boiler in the woods.

In Klamath Falls the waitress where he ate was Nita Webb, the farm girl who had left the little Oregon town of Dallas to see the world. She loved hearing stories of his experiences and he loved seeing her blue eyes light up as he told them. It blossomed into a romance.

Tom and Nita's decision to marry wasn't long in coming. Nita wrote her mother the news and the plans started taking shape for a wedding at the family home in Dallas. The entire Webb family gathered for the joyful occasion.

My mother's youngest brother, Larry, was home for the wedding, riding his first motorcycle. "Come on, Tom, try it out. It's a great machine," he coaxed his new brother-in-law. Of course Daddy, wanting to impress his new bride and in-laws, rose to the occasion. It was different than anything he had ever dealt with, but he climbed on that mechanical steed.

The ride he took carried him through the cabbage patch, over the neatly hilled rows of potatoes, narrowly missing a tree, and ended up against the chicken-yard fence. Those fine old Plymouth Rock hens squawked to high heaven, trying to fly up into the trees to get away from the strange, noisy machine that was invading their territory.

In spite of the path of destruction left in its wake, both Daddy and the motorcycle sustained only minor scratches. Everyone had a good laugh. The adventure made such a lasting impression on Daddy that he never again got involved with any machine with less than four wheels.

After the nuptials, my father and mother moved to Ryderwood, Washington, where Tom worked firing boiler on a logging train. As he shoveled coal into the boiler his mind wandered back to the quiet streams teeming with fish, the crisp, clean bite of the wind as he mushed his dog team through the Canadian wilderness. His homesteading memories were very special to him. Nita listened in rapt silence to Tom's stories of the frontier lifestyle and they fired her imagination. They started saving and dreaming. Alaska seemed to fit the bill because since 1912 it had been a U.S. Territory. Fishing, trapping and mining sounded new, interesting and exciting.

It was Webb tradition that when a daughter had a baby, the Webb mother would board whatever conveyance necessary to be with her. So it was in July of 1925, when Gram got off of the bus in Ryderwood to be with my mother when her first child was born.

My arrival didn't slow my parents' plans down at all. The funds for the trip north were intact by the time I was eight months old, and we boarded the steamship *Northwestern* in Seattle with tentative plans to go to Fairbanks, probably influenced by the thoughts that someone had left a few gold nuggets laying around.

As the ship wound its way through the Inland Passage and across the Gulf of Alaska, Daddy talked with Alaskans who were returning from "stateside" visits. They discouraged him about taking his family to the tent city of Fairbanks. There were no houses available and winter temperatures plummeted to -50 degrees Fahrenheit.

They suggested the milder climate of lower Cook Inlet. Plans changed. Landing in Seward, we rode the train to Anchorage. After renting a house on Third Avenue for two weeks for $2.50 while we waited for the *Princess Pat*, we continued our journey down Cook Inlet to the little fishing village of Seldovia.

My first birthday was celebrated there with several other July children.

Chapter 2

Dark Clouds

My mother's diary tells about her feelings during those first days in Seldovia:

"I can't believe the kindness of these complete strangers. We were invited into their homes, given a warm meal and a bed for the night. The next day, a man came up to Tom on the street and asked if we would live in his house while he was fishing in Cordova for the summer. Then Mr. Young, at the store, introduced Tom to a man who put him to work at the wonderful wage of $3 per day. I can't believe we have a house and Tom has a job and we have only been here two days. It is such a young country, only fifty-nine years, I feel we can grow with it. It has only had its own flag for the last 4 years."

These were happy days for my folks. They had found the land of their dreams, work to sustain them and wonderful new friends. My little brother, Leland Thomas, was born that February. All was well in the Shelford household.

My mother wrote glowing, enthusiastic reports of her new life to her family in Oregon. This inspired her brothers, Larry and Gardo Webb, to come north to trap that winter.

Seldovia was a picturesque little settlement built on a rocky hillside that dropped off to the shoreline of Seldovia Bay. Its main artery was a sturdy boardwalk built on piling that ran a mile along the waterfront. Sadly, the 1964 earthquake and tidal wave changed this in later years. The stores and canneries were built on the bay side of the walk on pilings, with the tide coming and going beneath them. On the other side of the walkway, the houses clung tenaciously to the rocky hillside or snuggled down in the more hospitable little valleys.

I have been told that I followed my father everywhere. When he would spit snoose over the rail I would stick my head between the side rails of the boardwalk and do my best to spit too. Who knows, if our lives hadn't taken a turn I might have attained world acclaim as a champion spitter after starting at such a tender age.

It seemed our lives were filled with endless sunshine. But into each life some rain must fall. The first signs of bad weather came when my mother started having headaches and fainting spells. The local doctor had no remedy for this condition. Daddy was panic stricken and sent us to Dallas to my grandparents where she could have proper medical attention. He would trap for the winter then come to bring us home to Alaska in the spring. With sad tears of parting, we left Seldovia and my dad.

My second birthday was on the southbound boat, complete with yellow crepe paper hats with blue tassels on top, a big cake with two candles and crew and passengers all singing "Happy Birthday."

My mother and grandparents had a little trouble converting me to "stateside." I insisted that my grandma's cow was a moose. My mother patiently explained to me that it was a cow but I insisted: "No, mama, it says its name all the time, "Moose, moose."

Sounded logical to me.

The agony of separation showed clearly in the loving letters that flowed throughout the winter between my parents. My mother cherished them and kept them in a special treasure box with mirrors on the sides that was topped with a soft jade green velvet lid. We were never to touch it.

True to his word, Daddy came to Oregon in the spring. He told us fascinating tales of his successful trapping and was anxious to get back to Seldovia for the commercial fishing season. In a flurry of excitement the packing began.

We did take time for walks. My parents would hold hands as we walked along. Daddy carried me on his shoulders when I got tired. Mother would carry my little brother, Leland.

Leland was seventeen months old now. Old enough to run and play. We spent many happy hours playing on the big front porch of my grandparents' home. I don't remember ever fighting, but being normal kids we probably did. But on the horizon, the storm clouds were darkening....

My mother was packing; Daddy was sitting on the bed holding me on his lap, talking to her. Leland was toddling around. The top tray of the trunk, holding the medical supplies that were always kept on hand in those days, was set out on a chair for a moment while my mother put things in the bottom part.

The next few minutes are indelibly imprinted on my mind and they changed our lives forever.

Suddenly, Leland had the carbolic acid bottle! When Daddy saw him he had pulled the cork out and was holding the bottle to his lips. Daddy dumped me on the floor and seized the bottle. Leland gasped, inhaling the deadly fumes. Everything from then on was an exercise in futility.

I sat very still in my little rocking chair where my dad put me, my hands folded in my lap. I was as frightened as a two-and-half-year old child could be.

It was five miles to town, no car, or phone, and I don't believe anything would have made a difference. Gram and my mother gave him raw eggs and did all of the things that could be done, but he had inhaled, not swallowed, the lethal dose.

In minutes my mother held my brother's lifeless body in her arms, as she sobbed terrible, wracking sobs. Daddy and Gram tried to comfort her, but she was inconsolable. Daddy was the one who finally remembered about me. He took me from my little rocking chair and held me.

We knelt beneath the oak trees in the Dallas cemetery by such a little mound of flowers. My mother's misery over the loss was heartbreaking to see. Tears rolled down her cheeks as she fixed breakfast, as she talked in a normal voice, as she went methodically about her daily duties. She didn't tell me silly made up stories to make me laugh any more. Her blue eyes held such pain, that you felt you should whisper in the presence of such agony.

I missed my little brother. I had no one to play with. My memories of him are limited as I was so young. Only one incident sticks in my mind. We wore little undershirts that our mother made for us from bleached flour sacks. They buttoned down the back. Leland and I were trying to dress ourselves one morning and, of course, couldn't reach the buttons. I convinced him that if we turned around fast enough we could do it. The end result was we got dizzy and fell into a giggling heap on the floor.

Many years later I asked my father, "How do people get through such pain and misery?"

He looked out the window wistfully with tears of memory gathering in his eyes. "You stand up straight and put one foot ahead of the other."

I know it works.

Chapter 3

A Terrible Loss and Coping

It was time for my folks to revamp their plans as the ticket money for the return trip to Alaska had gone for funeral expenses. Instead of going home to Alaska we went to the Okanogan country in northern Washington State where Uncle Bill was running an apple orchard.

He gave my Dad a job and a cabin for us to stay in for the summer. In the years that followed, I would come to feel toward this aunt and uncle as my second parents. Their daughter, Merlie, always seemed more like a sister than a cousin.

I loved the time we spent in the orchard with its wonderful irrigation ditches. In the summertime it gets to be 110 in the shade up in that part of the Okanogan country. In my young mind I associated the irrigation ditches with bathing. Hanging my every article of clothing on the lowest limb of an apple tree so as to not get them wet, I splashed happily up and down the ditch. What fun! That is, until my Uncle Bill saw me and ruined everything by telling my mother.

"Nita, did you want Wilma running naked up and down the irrigation ditch?" he asked.

My mother ran out and cut short my bathing program. She also impressed upon my mind, approaching the situation from the other end with a small switch, that this was not being done in the better circles.

Although her reprimand was very definite, I was not completely cured. She bought me a pair of shiny black patent leather shoes, the kind that came above the ankle, with straps that buttoned across the front. They were shiny. They reminded me of the rubber overshoes my dad wore over his shoes when it rained.

"Hmmm," I thought, "Maybe I could walk on water with them." Wrong! Did my mother appreciate my wonderful theories? Not at all.

Fall came and the orchard work was over. Daddy found a job eight miles west of Winthrop, Washington, at Fender's Mill. I was three that summer and my memories become clearer.

There were two cabins, a larger house, and a cook house, at the mill. We moved into one of the cabins. Charley and Louise Sullivan lived in the cabin next door. The cabins were not very impressive on the outside. They were made of rough lumber, covered with black tar paper held on by battens.

Our cabin had two bare little rooms. My mother attacked the situation with vigor, making it homey by putting up bleached flour-sack curtains. Around the edge of them she had crocheted wide yellow borders of lace in an intricate pattern. The hand-pieced quilts for the beds were not only colorful, but great for rainy afternoons when my mother would sit me on the bed saying, "Now see how many of the pieces you can tell me where they came from."

I loved that game and would say, "That one came from my best dress that you made for me. This one is from your dress," and so on.

Daddy made a table. I can't remember what it was made of because my mother covered it with a table cloth that she embroidered along the edge with yellow roses.

There was a dressing table in the bedroom. When I investigate it in my mind's eye it was two homemade shelves attached to the wall, but my mother put a flour-sack skirt around it with more embroidered roses. It may sound as though there were a lot of flour sacks but all bread was homemade or you didn't have any where we lived, and you never wasted any material.

Sitting on top was a glass container with face powder in it and a pincushion full of shiny pins. The pincushion was oblong, with pink flowers embroidered in satin stitch and filled with sawdust from the mill. The dressing table seemed very high. I even had to climb onto the bed to reach the powder to powder my nose and to touch the slick flowers on the pincushion. My usually helpful mother was no help whatsoever in this project. In fact she kept taking me down off the bed.

Behind the cabin was an outhouse that had cracks between the boards. It was fun to peek out through the cracks in the summer. But in the winter, the blowing snow would filter in through the cracks, making a very cold seat. Our water came from a creek about a hundred feet from the house.

At night, the timber wolves howled out their woes from the nearby woods. I don't remember being frightened of them because my mom and dad held me up to the window to see the wolf on top of the hill, silhouetted against the night sky. My mother explained that he was singing me a lullaby. I felt safe and secure. Besides how many kids have wolves to sing them a lullaby?

A few years ago I took my father in the motorhome for a brief journey down memory lane. The mill was a shambles, the cabins were gone, and the trees much taller than in my memory. We walked slowly around the area, trying to determine where our cabin had been. I kept walking back and forth, remembering the angle that we watched the wolf from the window of the cabin. Suddenly I stumbled on an old foundation post.

"You're right!" my dad said, "How could you possibly remember where the cabin stood? You were so little." He laughed when I told him how I remembered.

From our time at the mill, one little girl stands out in my memory. She was a very spoiled little girl like the Nellie Olson from "Little House on the Prairie." One sunny afternoon, several other mill family children and I were playing in the sand along the creek bank, building sand castles when the "Nellie" girl came riding up on a shiny red tricycle with a big teddy bear clutched in one arm. We stared in fascination at these luxurious things. In the midst of the Great Depression of the late '20s not many people could afford to give their children special toys. For a moment she paused for effect, then said in a nasty tone, "I have a *new* teddy bear and a *new* tricycle and you kids don't have any."

It was my first experience with deliberate rudeness. It took a minute for it to sink in.

"So, isn't that just great?" I said with complete lack of enthusiasm and returned to my play.

Since she hadn't gotten the attention she wanted by her entrance and announcement she rode her lovely new tricycle across our sand castles, leaving complete devastation in her wake.

It was noon time and several mothers chose this tense moment to call their children home for dinner, including the "Nellie" girl. In trying to get her tricycle turned around, she threw her teddy bear down, dragged her trike through the remains of our sand castle and left.

I sat alone in the sand, with the teddy bear laying where she had left it. I pondered the situation. I already knew you didn't take other people's things. Not even bratty kids' things. As I sat there digging a little hole, it came to my mind that I didn't remember anyone saying you couldn't bury them.

That wonderful thought gave me lots of enthusiasm and I dug the hole both wide and deep. I surveyed my handiwork with a critical eye, looked this way and that for any passers-by, then satisfied that it was safe, I slowly edged the teddy down to a comfortable resting place and returned the dirt to the hole. As a final measure, I ran back and forth over the area to destroy any evidence of digging. Feeling it was a job well done, I ran home.

Later "Mrs.Olson" came to our cabin with little "Nellie" in tow.

"Does your little girl have my little girl's NEW teddy bear?" My mother turned to me:

"Do you have her teddy bear?"

Consider the question.

"No, I don't have it," I said as I wrapped my doll carefully in her blanket, being far too busy to have any eye contact with my mother.

Later my mother was quiet and seemed to be thinking. Oh-oh. She reworded the sentence.

"Do you know where Nellie's teddy is?"

Well, that was different and you can't lie to your mother. I confessed and we all went to the "teddy bear cemetery" and did a great deal of digging. The good news was we never did find that silly bear. Mean little "Nellie" howled out her woes to her mother, who gave me a withering glance and reassured her child, "Don't cry Honey, Mommy will get you another, bigger teddy bear."

I got a severe scolding from my mother but I really felt it was worth it.

About this time my mother began to smile again and make little clothes that didn't fit anyone at our house. It was great to have her happy and telling me stories. My dad looked at her with such warmth it made our whole world beautiful. He was happier too. I would run to the door when he came from work. He would take my hands and let me stand on his feet as he walked us over to give my mom a kiss. It seemed that the rain had stopped falling in our lives.

My father woke me one night and took me to Sullivan's house next door. I liked these people. I got to sleep on three kitchen chairs put together with pillows on them. This was a new adventure, sleeping on kitchen chairs, and I hardly paid any attention to my parents' speedy departure.

The following day Daddy came and we drove to a house that was used for a hospital in Winthrop. There, he lifted me up to see a very tiny new baby and then took me to see my mother.

"What do you think of that new baby sister?" she asked, smiling.

"I think she is cute," I answered, thinking it was a good thing that she was coming to live at our house as she looked about the right size for all of those clothes my mother had been making.

"I want you to take good care of her," Mother said, quite seriously.

"Who is going to take care of Wilma?" Daddy asked, going along with the little game.

"Don't you worry about her. She will take care of herself."

Often I have thought about that conversation. My mother may have seen a spark of an independent nature in me, but I surely did need her badly.

They named the new baby Lolomi Margaret. The name "Lolomi" was from a book my mother had read. The Margaret was after our grandmother, who was very pleased. She wrote Loma a letter, welcoming her little namesake.

Daddy brought them home from the hospital, but my mother stayed in bed most of the time. It was a struggle for her to get up to comb my long curls. Neighbors dropped by to help with things and looked concerned.

One day my mother let me go to play with the Reeves children who lived in the bigger house down close to the mill. The cook house where their mother worked as cook was right next door. I had to be back at noon.

There were five children. Ralph was ten years old and watched the younger kids while his mother worked next door. I played with the kids and we fed the baby little bites of peaches that were cut up fine — no Gerber baby food in those days. She was in a jumper swing. I still couldn't tell time, so Ralph told me when it was noon and I ran home.

Later that afternoon, my mother was reading to me when she noticed little burned pieces of paper drifting past the window.

"Wilma, go to corner by Sullivan's house and look down the road. See what is causing those ashes." I ran quickly, being proud to be sent on a mission. I could hardly believe my eyes. Reeves' house was totally engulfed in flames. I ran panting back to my mother.

"Mama, Mama it's Reeves' house! I have to go to help the kids!" I cried.

"No! There are big people there, aren't there?" she asked in a firm voice.

"Yes. They have water buckets and they are handing them to each other but I don't see the kids."

When the smoke cleared, Louise Sullivan came to tell us only Ralph had survived. He had put the younger children down for their nap and was sitting in the kitchen when he smelled smoke. Opening the bedroom door, flames leaped out at him singeing his hair. He ran to alert his mother.

When the flames died down the little piles of ashes told the story of how the kids had played with matches and caught the bedding on fire. Then, growing more frightened, they had dragged the baby from her crib and taken her under the bed with them to get away from the flames. This explained why the father was unable to find the baby in her crib when he dashed into the fire, attempting to save his children. He had been so badly burned that he had to be hospitalized. My mother held me close and we cried.

My mother didn't seem to get any better and one day she sent me next door to get Louise Sullivan. It is hard to remember what happened next. Everything was very confusing for a three-and-half-year-old. They took my mother away. Someone contacted my father who was out in the woods working. He dropped everything and hurried to the hospital. When he arrived, my mother was lying with a sheet pulled over her face.

Gram came from Dallas on the train and I was glad to see her. She packed up our clothes with tears streaming down her face. We got on the train. I was excited about the ride on the train because I got to carry my little green satchel with the rabbits painted on the side that I kept my sewing in.

This was fun for awhile, then I said, "Gram, I want my mother now."

"I'm sorry, Wilma. Your mother is here but she is in the baggage coach ahead." Again there were tears. I didn't understand what was going on, but I knew my mother loved me too much to go away and not come back, so I didn't worry too much.

Her death was caused by a doctor drinking and neglecting to check things carefully when my sister was born. It had caused gangrene and eventually hemorrhaging. It took just twenty-four days to do its deadly work. The headstone beneath the oak trees she loved, next to Leland, in the Dallas cemetery read:

NITA MAY WEBB SHELFORD
BORN JANUARY 28, 1905
DIED MARCH 3, 1929
BELOVED WIFE AND MOTHER

It was not until two years later that I got it through my head that it was not in her power to come home to us. I had a dream one night.

The Standard Oil truck making daily deliveries to Falls City came by Gram's house. There was no bus so anyone coming to visit rode the truck from Dallas. I dreamed my mother was coming home and would be on the truck. I was very excited. I jumped out of bed and ran to tell Gram the good news.

With pain in her eyes she tried to tell me that could never be, but I wouldn't listen. I hope someplace there is forgiveness for the agony I put Gram through that day. I put on my favorite blue dress, combed my hair and ran to sit on the steps by the mailbox to wait. Soon I saw the truck coming and I ran to the edge of the road. The driver waved, little dust clouds curled up behind the wheels. The truck rolled out of sight.

At last the sick realization that she could never come home was clear to me. I lay on the ground beneath the Japanese quince bush, sobbing my heart out until Gram came and led me back to the house. I did a lot of growing up that day — accepting things as they were. If you've got it to do, get on with it.

Daddy had gone to the funeral and then back to Winthrop to his job, leaving my baby sister and me with our grandparents. The Shelford family financial situation, which had not been great in the first place, had been badly strained by hospital and funeral expenses and left him no choice in the matter.

About a month later, fate dealt him another cruel blow. While he was in the woods working, his cabin burned to the ground. Sitting on a stump that evening staring at the smoldering remains, he made the decision to go back to Alaska. He showed up at Gram's house with only the clothes on his back and his last paycheck in his pocket. I was delighted and much too young to realize he had come to Dallas to say goodbye to my sister and me.

He rocked my sister that night and looked sadly at her as she slept in his arms, then he tucked me in bed and read me a story. When I awoke in the morning he was gone. Many years would pass before I would see him again. Gram received letters and money from him now and then. My grandparents were good to us, and fed us, but home as I had known it was a thing of the past.

Chapter 4

Farm Days

The years spent on the farm in Dallas were happy years. Loma and I ran over those Oregon hills picking wild flowers for Gram. There were so many different kinds in the spring, lovely white Trilliums, delicate Lady Slippers, spicy fragrant Pinks (wild carnations) and bright yellow Johnny-jump-ups. We found wild strawberries on the hillside and black caps further out in the woods. The fruit orchard and the acre of garden kept us blissfully unaware that there was a depression going on.

Loma and I helped in the garden, carried in wood, fed chickens and gathered eggs. But my favorite chore was going after the cows at milking time in the evening. I would walk out over the hills calling, "So bossy, so bossy," and usually Echo would answer with a long "moo." Echo was the oldest, a gentle Jersey with a fawn-like face. Her daughter, Lady Valentine, looked like her mother but surely didn't have her mother's sunny disposition. Echo must have been traveling in bad company when she conceived that miserable little rascal. Lady Valentine was definitely a nonconformist. When the rest of the cows headed for the barn she would get some wild idea, and with tail flying high, run off in some other direction. I walked many an extra mile for that heifer, through the berry bushes and poison oak.

I finally came upon a more persuasive method. I rode her home. At least that way I knew where she was. I took a piece of rope along and when I got close enough to her I would slip a loop over her head and jump aboard. If she looked any other direction but down the road I rapped that side of her head with the knot in the end of the rope. All of the cows would get into the act, and we would come stampeding down the hill. Well, that is, as stampedy as a bunch of milk cows could get. As I came through the barnyard gate, I would grab the overhead piece above the gate and swing from my trusty steed.

I was very proud of my labor-saving ingenuity and good cowmanship until Granddad hollered at me for running the cows. He wanted to know how Lady Valentine got that rope around her neck. Hmmm.

When Granddad milked Lady Valentine, she would invariably try to kick the milk pail over. In order to anticipate her next move he had to put his head against her flank to feel her tense up to kick, then grab the bucket and stand back.

Fawny also got milked. She was a nice cow and often I would walk beside her on our homeward journey with my arm over her neck, telling her about my busy day. She was good company and that's something I didn't have much of. Maisy and Brownie were still little calves. I was allowed to play with them in the yard, as long as I watched them closely and took them back to the pen afterward.

Every one of them, except Echo, I had weaned. I would mix mash in a bucket of milk, put my hand down into the milk and stick a finger up. The calves would try to suck my finger and in this way learned to drink from the bucket.

We didn't have much money, but we were never hungry. Every morning we had oatmeal mush for breakfast topped with thick cream skimmed from the top of the crock of milk. The milk was cooled in a screened cupboard on the back porch in crockery containers. Nobody had a refrigerator in those days. Some people in the city had ice boxes they put block ice in to keep things cool, but we didn't have money for anything like that. Sometimes, for breakfast variety, Gram would put several cups of wheat in a slow cooker overnight. The slow cooker was a well-insulated, thick round container about two feet tall that was heated by round stone-like disks. These disks were put on the back of the stove to heat in the afternoon. When dinner was over in the evening Gram would place them inside of the cooker. The wheat would be put into a container, covered with water then the tight lid would be put in place.

This container was set into the big insulated cooker and the cooker lid secured. In the morning the results were delicious and my favorite breakfast.

Granddad played banjo and guitar. In the cool of the summer evenings Gram, Loma and I would sit on the front porch shelling peas or snapping green beans for canning the next morning, and listen to him play and sing the old songs. He didn't, however, appreciate it when Loma and I sang along. It might have been that what we lacked in musical knowledge, we made up for in volume and enthusiasm. The songs he sang are dear to me: "Strawberry Roan," "Miss Fogarty's Xmas Cake," and sad ones like "Darlin' Nellie Gray."

Gram couldn't afford children's bedtime story books but, instead, she read to us out of our mother's scrapbook of poems. As a result of this choice of literature I could rattle off "Oh young Lochinvar has come out of the west" at four instead of knowing all about "Little Red Riding Hood." I loved Robert Service too. My favorite was "Dangerous Dan Magrew," with "The Cremation of Sam McGee" running a close second.

Each summer I was allowed to go to my Aunt Millie and Uncle Bill's place. Their daughter, Merlie, was five years older than I with blond hair and mischievous brown eyes. I thought she was wonderful because she thought up such interesting things to do. We rode double over the countryside on a retired race horse called "Fleet."

Aunt Millie was always trying to make Merlie and me a little more ladylike and a bit less tomboyish. Her efforts were noble but futile. For example, Merlie and I always looked forward to making the mile and a half trip to the mailbox on horseback. My aunt's idea was to saddle and bridle the horse and sit very straight, looking a little pained that we were subjected to this sort of activity. If she could have found a sidesaddle for us, I have no doubt she would have been pleased.

Our idea was a little different: halter and lead rope, climb on at the barn loading dock, give Fleet a rousing swat on the backside, holler like a Comanche, bend low over the horse's mane, and fly past the house at such a speed that we could honestly say we didn't hear Aunt Millie shouting at the top of her voice from the front porch.

When we weren't riding the horse, we did constructive things like make a harness for the goat out of my uncle's leather strapping that he kept on hand to mend the horses' harness. We used lots of the shiny copper rivets, not only to keep the harness together but to make it pretty. I think we suspected Uncle Bill wouldn't like our ingenuity, as I don't remember running to show him the finished product.

Once the harness was completed, we made a cart out of a prune box with the two back wheels off an old trike. Surveying our handiwork, we decided it was time to try them out.

We harnessed the nervous nanny goat to the cart. Then Merlie suggested I get in, just to see if it seemed all right. As I crouched in the cart, she swatted the goat across the backside. Goat, cart and I flew off at top speed across the irrigation ditches. Each crossing bounced the cart to new and perilous heights. My ear-piercing objections were voiced at such volume they brought my uncle from the other end of the filbert orchard.

Someplace along that journey, I got a glimpse of Merlie leaning against a tree with tears running down her cheeks. Surely she could not be laughing that hard at a time like this!

Chapter 5

Goodbye Echo

I was at Laurelwood with Aunt Millie and Uncle Bill in 1934 when the neighbors from down the hill who had a telephone came up with the message that my grandfather had passed away. I was nine.

Again our lives made a major change. Gram had to sell the place because she couldn't manage it alone. It was a hard decision for her to make as she had lived there for 17 years and her friends were there. The sale of the place meant the stock had to go too.

Echo was gentle and not hard to catch, but the younger ones wouldn't let other people near them. Gram came after me, where I was sitting under the oak tree crying, and told me to go get the cows. I felt like Judas, calling "Come Lady Valentine, come Maizy, come Fawny." They all came, nuzzling me and wanting to be scratched, even that miserable Lady Valentine. I walked into the trailer that was to transport them. They followed me. I never saw them again. My heart was breaking. It was a sad day.

We moved to a house that my Uncle Gardo owned in West Salem, Oregon. Even though we only moved 12 miles away, it was a different world. There was no orchard to run and pick a juicy apple or pear from. The cows that were my friends and their wonderful rich milk were gone. We got little bottles of milk from the store now when there was money for it. The big garden we had pulled the armloads of carrots from for canning was gone.

The friends who had known my mother and who had always been part of my life were far away. Gone was the country school with only eight children attending, where my mother before me had also been a student. Now I was just a strange little country kid, in a classroom of thirty kids in the same grade. My grandmother made my clothes like the ones she had worn as a child. The gray striped outing flannel, high-waisted dresses were a constant source of amusement to the other children. There wasn't money for tap dancing lessons or piano lessons like the other children. Although I didn't feel deprived, I simply did not have anything to talk to them about.

I knew no one would understand how I missed Maizy's cold nose nuzzling me to be petted or the chickens flying to meet me when I came out with the bucket of feed. How much fun it was to walk along the rows in the garden watching to see first sprouts. I missed my swing that hung from a log cross piece in the top of tall fir trees that my Uncle Larry had put up for me. I made the sad mistake of saying how I missed the farm and the other children laughed and said. "She is lonesome for her friends the cows."

It was a low spot in my life. It was senseless to want things because it was so futile, but the one thing I couldn't help wanting was a bike. If I could even push someone else's bike, I was thrilled. I maintained good grades, got along well with my teachers, but had no personal friends. I can never remember being so unhappy and discouraged in my life.

It was here in West Salem that I first heard radio and began to realize there was a world beyond. In the evening after our homework was completed we were allowed to listen to "Amos and Andy" or "Gang Busters." I laughed at George Burns & Gracie Allen and Fibber McGee & Molly. When "Innersanctum" came on, Loma and I huddled together as the sound effects of the creaking door came from the speaker. If someone would have said "boo," I am sure we would have gone through the roof. That was fun, but I still missed the farm.

Uncle Larry came home from the Navy after putting seven and half years aboard the *USS Omaha*. He brought a buddy, Ted Rhodabach, with him. Ted's family were all gone and he became a member of ours. He called Gram "Ma" and treated her like a very thoughtful son should. Ted and Larry supplied groceries and life got a little easier. Gram put in a small garden, about 20 feet square, and Loma and I pulled weeds and watered it. Later, Larry and Ted spaded up an area about 50 by 100 that gave us room for corn and tomatoes too. Things were better.

They also bought Gram her first electric washing machine. She was excited but accepted it on a limited basis. She washed sheets, towels and dish towels in it, but for anything that was really soiled, like socks or shirt collars, out came the old faithful wash board.

Larry was the one bright spot in that period of my life. Tall with gray-blue eyes that twinkled with mischief, he was blessed with a real zest for living. He arrived home from the Navy driving a Model A Ford with a rumble seat. It seemed he always sensed the things that delighted Loma and me, like letting us ride to the store in that wonderful rumble seat.

Later, he sold the car and bought a big red Harley Davidson motorcycle. Riding behind Larry on that big Harley was the thrill of a lifetime. Gram didn't approve of "that crazy machine" or the fact that Ted and Larry sometimes indulged in a little nip of strong spirits while riding it.

She felt justified in her feelings early one morning when a taxi brought Larry home. He was so completely swathed in bandages that he looked like a mummy, but he smelled more like a brewery. When we had helped him into the house Grandma asked him what happened.

"Well, there were three corners, Ma, and I only took two of them."

After that she didn't talk to him for a long time. I fed him meals until he could take enough bandages off his hands that he could hold a spoon. Some times Stella Cook would come over from next door to visit and would feed him. I often wondered, if I hadn't fed him, if Gram would have let him starve, like she said he so richly deserved.

In 1934, we received a letter from Alaska. Daddy had remarried. He asked if Gram and us girls wanted to come to Alaska. Gram asked us how we felt about it. I couldn't remember what Daddy looked like, even when I tried hard. I didn't hurt anymore missing him. Loma had no memories of him at all. Gram's friends were all in Oregon. We all voted no. With that decision it would be many years until I saw Daddy again.

Chapter 6

Walla Walla

In 1936, Aunt Millie and Uncle Bill asked us to come to Walla Walla, Washington, and live with them. It was time to make a move. The decision was made to accept their generosity. On July 2 my Uncle Bill and Merlie came to West Salem to pick us up. I don't think I even looked back. I just breathed a sigh of relief.

It was dark when we got to Walla Walla and I was anxious for it to be morning so I could see my new home. When dawn came I was so excited. It was the beginning of one of the happiest periods of my life.

The first special thing that happened was I was allowed to learn to ride Merlie's bike. It was a beautiful silver Hawthorn Duralium with steer-horn handlebars. Although it was 105 degrees in the shade and I was prone to getting nose bleeds in hot weather, nothing could slow me down now that I had a chance to ride a bike. I was in seventh heaven.

On my birthday, the 16th day of July, I was surprised and excited when Loma and I both got our first bicycles. The bicycles were not only for pleasure. Every day we would be riding three miles each way to the little Adventist church school. For the next several years the bicycles would play a very important part in our lives.

Merlie had a six-mile ride each way to school in College Place. Once in a while, when the weather was really impossible, she was allowed to take the family car, a Model A Ford sedan.

Although there was little money, Aunt Millie took one look at the gray outing-flannel dresses that had caused us so much embarrassment and started making a presentable wardrobe for Loma and me. Aunt Millie would sit down in her big chair and get out the Sears and Roebuck catalog. Loma, Merlie and I would gather around as she turned the pages to the dress section.

"Oh I like that dress!" one of us would say, but it cost $2.50. That was a lot of money in those days. If she thought it was practical, she would get out a newspaper, remove the cloth from the dining table, look at the picture in the catalog and cut a pattern out of newspaper. On Saturday night we would make that weekly shopping trip to town. With Aunt Millie's knowledgeable guidance the material would be selected for 0 or 15 cents per yard. Before the week was out the miracle had happened! We had dresses that looked like the ones we had admired in the catalog.

My aunt and uncle's house was on the ranch my uncle managed. It was a white, two story, saltbox type. The kitchen curtains were bleached flour sacks, neatly starched and hemmed. Bright yellow daffodils marched across the lower border. This was accomplished with carbon paper to trace the flowers on to the curtains, crayons to color them, and finally setting the color with a hot flatiron. This lasted until they were washed. Then you had to do it all over again. I loved the bright colors and the activities.

There was a big garden to hoe. Merlie and I would often be there by 4 a.m. It was better to do it then, before the temperature soared later in the day.

I loved the apple orchard and, since my uncle was the foreman, I was given a job carrying drinking water to the crew during picking or thinning season. There was no piped water and the water in the irrigation ditches would be contaminated with arsenic from the spray used on the trees. I got my first check at the rate of $1.00 per 10-hour day, and it went to help with household expenses.

During the next few years I worked driving team on the spray rig in spraying season. I was proud when I was allowed to harness the team and took the job very seriously. The only time I remember being reprimanded was one lovely spring day when I took the team in at noon.

We were spraying about 1/4 mile from the house. I had to water and feed the team before I could eat lunch, so getting in quickly was top priority. Solution: pull the pin on the double tree, jump on it and snap the reins. The horses knew they were headed for food and water and didn't need much encouragement. End result: a wonderful hair-raising ride balanced on the double tree bouncing along the dusty road. We made that 1/4 mile in record time. The problem arose when my aunt happened to observe me skidding around that last corner. Not at all ladylike, in her opinion and what's more she was horrified that I looked like I was enjoying it. (Oh perish the thought.) After that, when I came in view of the house, I would jump from the double tree and trot sedately along behind the horses trying to have the right pained expression to please my Aunt, whom I adored.

It was still depression times, although President Roosevelt had the New Deal going. The Work Project Administration, or WPA as it was commonly called, had swung into action along with the CCCs, Civilian Conservation Corps. We could begin to see the results on the countryside and in the attitude of the people. The needy people were able to work again and, believe me, nearly everyone was needy. Young as I was, I thought that "guy back there in Washington D.C." was showing amazingly good sense in his way of getting the rusty old wheels of progress in motion.

My uncle started to teach me to drive the truck in the orchard, but he was not cut out to teach a teenager to drive. He would hang onto the seat white knuckled, shouting: "Get over that way." "Go slower." "No, no, don't turn there." I would end up in tears and he would go home and take two aspirin. Thank goodness for Merlie. Every time we got away from the house, she would let me drive the Model A. By the time I was thirteen, my Uncle was amazed at what a good job he had done teaching me to drive.

We heard from Daddy in Alaska occasionally. Daddy's wife, Lydia, was running the Homer Post Office. Daddy was hauling the mail and freight from Seldovia with his boat the *Jungle Queen*. We had a new little brother. They had named him Leland Thomas, but called him Sonny. I was glad for Daddy. He had a lot of heartaches and it seemed at last his life was getting on a more even keel. Lydia was much better about writing than Daddy had ever been. She sent pictures of our northern section of family. She asked us to make out an order to Sears for school clothes and send it to her.

Gram missed Oregon, and in 1939 she and Loma went back. I stayed, and went to boarding school at Yakima Valley Academy in Granger, Washington. I was very homesick and even falling madly in love with the handsomest boy in school did not cure it. Glenn was tall and dark and had the saddest brown eyes. He had been in an accident in which his mother and sister had been killed shortly before coming to school. He was having a rough time dealing with it.

At that time, in Adventist schools, they did a very good job of keeping the boys and girls from having any contact with each other, so our love affair consisted mostly of notes. We did manage hand holding by the river and my very first grown-up kiss. I made the sad mistake of keeping the notes on top of my closet and they were discovered when a repair guy was fixing a light in our room. This young man not only read the notes, he seemed to feel it was his Christian duty to report the find. Oh boy, I was in real trouble.

Off to the office I went. My punishment was to be campus bound for the upcoming Thanksgiving holiday. I had planned on going home to visit and I was very homesick. That presented a major problem. I really didn't want to upset anyone, but I was definitely going home. I did. That ended my sojourn at YVA.

Glenn was good about writing and I missed him terribly. A problem arose. My aunt and uncle decided I shouldn't have the letters as they were too romantic for a 14-year-old. They read them to themselves, in front of me and laughed over the contents. I guess that is one thing I've never forgiven. If anyone touches my mail, even now, I get very upset. We managed to get a few messages through, and at camp meeting time I saw him. Although this relationship didn't stand the rigors of separation and time, don't underestimate the depth and the pain of teen-age love.

At 15 I was very tired of the long procession of people who told me what to do. Merlie was married and had moved to Colfax with her husband and son. I really missed them. I stayed in Walla Walla awhile and then joined Gram and Loma in Oregon.

I was restless. I had too much time on my hands and we were driving Gram to distraction.

One day in the spring of 1941, just after the mail came, Gram called Loma and me in and asked us to sit down. She sounded so serious that she immediately had our undivided attention.

"On the third of March you girls are going on the bus to Portland where you will have dinner with your dad's sister and family. You will then go on to Seattle, get on the Alaska Steamship *McKinley* and go to Alaska to live with your father."

Both Loma and I were shocked. I have often smiled during these past 55 years looking back at the statement I made then: "I am not going to that God-forsaken iceberg and if by any chance it should happen, I am certainly *not going to stay!*"

Chapter 7

North to Alaska

Just like in the movie, "A Yank at Eaton," when Mickey Rooney said, "I am certainly not going to England" and the next picture shows his face in the porthole, well, that's how things were with Loma and me. The next thing I knew we were walking up the gangplank of the *SS McKinley* at Pier 2 Seattle.

From Portland to Seattle was about a six-hour trip in those days. At six a.m. we were picked up at the Seattle bus station by one of the executives from the Alaska Steamship Company that Daddy had contacted. He took us to breakfast and delivered us to the boat. I tried to act gracious but I had the most awful headache. Buses do that to me.

Part of the headache may have been apprehension, as I was about to leave life as I knew it and there was nothing I could do about it. I wasn't afraid. Things were just totally out of my control and that is always unnerving.

Questions flooded my mind. What would my dad be like? I knew he was a fisherman, but the only fishermen I knew anything about were the ones I studied in the New Testament classes in school and church, who fished the Sea of Galilee. They wore long, flowing robes. Would Daddy like us? I could barely remember him, and Loma had no memories of him at all. She was only two months old when he returned to Alaska. Would Lydia like us or be the "wicked stepmother?"

Well if you've got it to do, get on with it.

Aboard the *SS McKinley* we were assigned a stateroom with three bunks. We soon found we had a roommate who was an attractive, well-dressed young lady, maybe five feet tall. Her pixie smile showed a dimple in her cheek and made her blue eyes sparkle. As she walked with us to the dining room she told us she was going to Kodiak. I was very surprised, several years later, to discover her profession. It would have set my father's teeth on edge had he known that his teen-age daughters were rooming with a prostitute. At the time we were all blissfully unaware and couldn't have had better company.

The weather was calm and cool as we slid across the glassy surface of Puget Sound. I lay perfectly still in my bunk, being sure I would get seasick if I moved. When we were three hours out I decided I was one of those lucky people who are not affected by motion sickness and that was true — well, at least as long as it was dead calm.

Loma, at this time, was twelve and already a couple of inches taller than my 5 feet 4 inches. Her blue eyes and dark brown hair were like our mother's side of the family, while mine leaned toward light auburn, perhaps more like the Welsh side. Often people would think she was older than me, which of course, at fifteen, provoked me to no end and amused her. Today, I would think it was great.

The dining room was very impressive with its sparkling glassware, white linen table cloths and stiffly starched waiters catering to our every need. After being raised to sit down, hush up and clean up our plate, this was heaven. I was sorry in later years when this fine old ship found its final resting place on a lonely stretch of beach in the Aleutian Islands.

There were dances aboard but we had never danced, so outside of walking by the salon on the deck and hearing the music we didn't go to them. With teen-age curiosity we walked by and heard the music but about that time a couple came on deck. The man had his arm around a girl and threw a beer bottle overboard. That was too much sin too close so we hurried off to our stateroom, where we giggled over our adventure.

About the time I was convinced I was pretty salty, we hit the tail end of a storm in Queen Charlotte Sound. Luckily we didn't arrive for the storm's full fury, because early on Loma and I began to find out what the word seasickness meant. The thing about seasickness that has always amazed me is that from death's door to reasonably good health just takes a little quiet water.

By the time we docked in Ketchikan we were feeling quite well and eager to get a look at our first Alaska city. We were poorly dressed for the freezing temperatures and blowing snow. Our dresses, saddle oxfords and anklets were fine in Oregon, but this was a whole different ball game. As the other passengers descended the gangplank and walked along the narrow streets, we followed. It was hard to keep our minds on the sights as the fine snow swirled about our bare legs. I know Lydia never suspected we didn't even own a pair of slacks or she would have seen to it that we did.

The boat docked at the main part of town. Dallas, Oregon, that we had just left is fairly flat country, so I was fascinated with the houses clinging to a hillside so steep you could have ground-level entrances on three floors. There were thick Spruce forests cloaking these abrupt ascents. We hurried from one store to the other to keep from spending too much time braving the elements. Our tour was for viewing purposes only, as we had very little money. The shoreside adventure was short and shivery, putting us back aboard in about two hours.

One of the advantages of slow old steamships that carried their freight loose in the hold, versus the new ferries with freight vans, was that the ship spent from three to twelve hours in each town, while the longshoremen unloaded freight one sling load at a time. This gave the passengers time to wander freely around each coastal town — economically good for the town and pleasant for the passengers.

There was a brief stop at Juneau, which, according to the information we gleaned, had been the capitol since 1906. The buildings clung to the hillside here also. When it got dark the lights from the town shone out across Gastineau Channel, making a memorable sight. Petersburg was a very brief stop while they unloaded the cannery supplies, and since it was at night, we saw little.

The Inside Passage is an interesting trip any time, with the lighthouses perched precariously on the rocky islands and shorelines.

From Cape Spencer to Hinchenbrook Island, the Gulf of Alaska was as peaceful as a mill pond, thank goodness, and we awoke after a week aboard ship to complete silence. I hurried onto the deck to find we were anchored in Resurrection Bay. Nestled along the shoreline was the little town of Seward. It was named, of course, for William Henry Seward who battled everyone in Washington, D.C., in order to purchase Alaska from Russia. This town is the southern terminus of the Alaska Railroad where I had landed fourteen years earlier with my parents.

It was here on the beach of Resurrection Bay in 1793 Russian sailors built the first ship constructed on the west coast of North America, and there had been some kind of a settlement there ever since. In 1941, the road only went out to Moose Pass 27 miles away but was not yet connected to the rest of the world except by trails and the railroad.

In Seward we transferred to the smaller ship *Cordova* and were assigned a stateroom. Since freight also was being transferred it gave us time to go explore the town and say good-bye to the Fairbanks and Anchorage passengers who were boarding the train to continue north.

In a little hole-in-the-wall soda fountain we ordered a Coke and had our first experience of hearing the phrase, "We are out, but it's on the boat." This phrase was very popular in the days when the steamships brought all of the supplies.

The *Cordova* was a combination passenger-freighter with only about a dozen staterooms, all opening onto the outside deck, and didn't break any speed records. The boat was still at the dock with winches grinding and groaning when we went to sleep, but we awoke to the boat's gentle rocking as we made our way toward Woman's Bay, Kodiak. When our roommate from the *McKinley* left the boat in Kodiak she gave us a reserved little dimpled smile and we gave her a hug.

Woman's Bay was the first place I ever saw fog roll over a mountain like thick cream pouring out of a pitcher. In a matter of minutes it reduced the visibility to zero. It looked like something out of a scary horror film. People twenty feet away became shadowy apparitions accompanied by voices.

By midafternoon the following day we were into Cook Inlet, where our first stop was Port Graham. The *Cordova* was too large to go to the dock in the village, so the anchor was dropped. A lifeboat was readied to take the one lady passenger ashore. I wish I could remember what the place looked like, but my eyes were glued to the lifeboat swinging in the davits being prepared for the journey ashore. I felt the boat we were on was small enough at 250 feet and that lifeboat looked to me like it was way too small to go out in all that water.

One of the ship's crew offered the lady a hand as she stepped from the deck into the boat but she smiled and, grasping the rail, swung a leg easily over the side of the lifeboat and seated herself. I was surprised at her agility as there were threads of silver in her black hair. She was tall and sat with her back straight, emanating a sense of natural dignity. The crewman climbed in and gave the signal to lower away.

I held my breath. The boat started to lower and then only one end was going down. One of the pulleys had hung up! The results were terrifying. The lowering process was stopped but the problem caused the boat to hang at an angle. Many would have panicked, but the lady simply braced her heels on a rib of the boat and calmly reached for the gunnel to steady herself. The boat had tipped so far that she was almost standing erect but was doing a lot better than I at that point. I had never been around boats. I watched white knuckled, gripping the railing and staring wide-eyed at the drama taking place before me. Shortly, the situation was corrected and they continued shoreward with the brave lady looking toward the group who were awaiting her on the beach. Their manner was unconcerned, as though they were used to hanging out over a frigid body of water.

Nearby, unbeknown to me, a man was watching my reactions. He came nearer and spoke to me.

"Aren't you headed for Homer?" he asked.

"Yes, we are." I answered hesitantly.

"Has anyone told you the bigger boats can only get about halfway across the bay before it gets too shallow for them? You have to row the last seven miles. I really thought you should know."

I searched his face for a trace of a smile, something that would tell me he was kidding, but he played it deadpan.

I thanked him weakly for the information and returned to my stateroom to think about this new development. He probably retreated to the bar to tell cute stories and have a good laugh about the young and gullible.

The arrival of the monthly winter boat to Seldovia was a big event. The dock was crowded with the townspeople as the longshoreman dropped the big hawsers over the piling. Loma and I stood at the railing, nervously searching the faces to find our stepmother's cousin whom we had never seen before. She was to meet us. Then a voice called, "Wilma, Loma, over here" and there was Juanita Berteson, waving.

She was dressed in warm slacks and a bright colored jacket. A matching scarf on her head left only bits of her light brown hair showing around her pleasant face. The warmth in her smile was a real comfort to two young girls in a strange country.

The winch creaked as it hoisted the gangplank into place. Loma and I walked down the gangplank carrying our suitcases. Looking around us, it didn't take long to decide dresses had a place but not in this country.

Then I saw the fishermen. Great! They didn't wear flowing robes! They wore white caps at a jaunty angle on the side of their heads, hip boots turned down and blue jeans. I was relieved they didn't look like the Galilee bunch.

It had been thirteen years since my mother and I had boarded the outgoing steamer here in Seldovia. My memories didn't go back that far as I was only two then. As Juanita walked us down the boardwalk toward her home, I was surprised when people would stop us and say, "You look like your mother," or "I remember when you followed your dad down the boardwalk as a little tyke."

Juanita guided us into the first store we came to saying, "I promised Mrs. Young we would stop by."

As we entered, an elderly lady came from behind the counter and greeted us warmly. After chatting a bit she said, "I have something for you, Wilma," and disappeared into her quarters. She returned momentarily, handing me a small white box. "Open it," she said with a smile.

I lifted the lid and saw a beautiful hand-embroidered table cloth. It had been embroidered with French knots in six-strand floss that emphasized the lilac pattern.

The edging was crocheted in a variegated lavender to match the lilacs. I stared at the lovely gift, trying to think of what to say.

Softly she said, "Your mother made this for me. When I heard about her passing away I put it away for you."

For one terrible moment I was afraid I would cry in front of all these strangers. Clutching my treasure tightly, I managed to thank her around the lump in my throat and give her a hug.

Old memories fluttered through my mind of my mother sitting and embroidering as I sat on my little green three-legged stool beside her, working on my sewing project. Once in a while she bent down to inspect my stitches.

The words from her diary came flooding back to me of the people's kindness and generosity. Darn, these people were making it hard to dislike this place properly.

"The dock in Homer has been damaged so bad by ice the *Cordova* can't tie up over there. John Colberg will take you into the slough on the *Copper* tomorrow after they get the Homer freight loaded on the scow," Juanita told us.

We met Juanita's husband, Russ, at dinner time. He stood over six feet tall and had broad shoulders and big brown eyes that twinkled with mirth. This man's sense of humor has become a matter of history in these parts but, of course, at the time I was not aware of that.

"Do you remember your dad?" he asked me.

"I think so, but it has been a long time." He smiled with what I thought was understanding.

"Oh, you won't have any trouble recognizing him. He has a long white beard, one of those ship's horns and a lantern he swings back and forth as he calls, 'Halloo the ship.' You'll know him right away." and he nodded his head reassuringly.

"Well now," I thought as I mulled over my accumulated information. "I will have to row the last seven miles of the trip to Homer in a skiff, according to the man on the *Cordova,* and my father 'halloos' the ship. Tomorrow is going to truly be a day to remember."

That evening Juanita cooked a wonderful dinner and afterward we sat around visiting. The following morning she walked us down to the dock where we nervously climbed down the ladder (I hate dock ladders) onto the *Copper*. Loma didn't say anything about it worrying her, but as far as that goes, I didn't say anything either. Juanita waved as we chugged down Seldovia Bay on the little fishing boat.

The scow was anchored on the far side of Seldovia Bay and we picked it up on the way out. It was piled so high with Homer freight it looked like a floating mountain. Lawrence Ohlson was decking and he quickly secured the scow and the journey began.

Loma and I sat down in the galley. I hadn't shared the matter with her about the rowing so I worried alone as we slowly made our way straight across Kachemak Bay to the slough. The weather was sunny and calm.

Lawrence finished his deck work and came down into the galley. Reaching into a sack on the table he took out a loaf of uncut homemade bread. He pulled a hunting knife of breath-taking size from his scabbard and cut the loaf longways three times. A can of Spam followed, also cut crossways into three healthy slices. Placing a couple of these hefty slices of Spam between two of the long slices of bread he started to take a bite, then turned and said, "Do you kids want a sandwich?"

Never had I seen a sandwich made in this manner. We declined in shaky little voices. He then poured a half cup of coffee, pulled a bottle from his pocket and filled the cup with whiskey. Oh my! In Adventist schools we had been taught that "when the demon alcohol is upon a man, he is completely without reason." Perhaps he would be the one who threw us into the skiff and set us adrift to row the other seven miles. That was a very long two-hour journey. However, in the second hour, after passing the halfway mark and we were still aboard the *Copper* I breathed a sigh of relief. I thought a lot about the man who had given me the rowing report. Miserable wretch.

As we approached the slough entrance, Lawrence shortened the tow line and stood by with the ax, for what I didn't know. I later learned he would have cut the scow loose if it beached while we were making entry into the slough but I didn't know it then. He wasn't really acting dangerous but I still worried because I had seen him take a drink. I watched him carefully until he put the ax away.

Once we were inside of the slough I saw a knot of people standing on the shore. Scanning the group anxiously, I spotted Daddy and Sonny. I knew him instantly, in spite of the "halloo the ship" story. "Loma, do you see that man up there in the white fisherman's cap standing by that Model A Ford truck? See that little boy with him?"

"Yes."

"That's Daddy and Sonny," I said, and from somewhere out of the dim distant past came that warm feeling that if Daddy was there everything would be okay. It had been a very long time since I had felt that way.

Chapter 8

Homer's Sunny Shores

John maneuvered the scow skillfully into the slough's narrow opening and against the sandy beach where it could be unloaded easily. The boat itself was now beside a beached skiff. Daddy and Sonny were standing by to help us ashore.

Lawrence, whom I felt more comfortable around since he wasn't carrying a hatchet, brought our suitcases from the boat. They were put into the back of Daddy's battered, black Model A Ford truck, then Dady slid in under the steering wheel. Loma sat in the middle, and I sat next to the door holding Sonny, who fidgeted a bit nervously. He really didn't know me and was not exactly sure what to say to half-grown sisters that suddenly sprouted up in his life. He scooted up as close to the front window as possible, sitting on the very tip of my knees, trying desperately to think of something to say. Finally he turned around and said in a burst, "Joe Hill had a bar in Seldovia and it burned and it made so much smoke that you could see it clear over here." We all laughed at this outburst of information and I gave him a hug.

Sonny was five years old and I was a little surprised he was not more territorial. Most children's reaction to having their stronghold invaded is to feel threatened and be obnoxious. Instead he was considerate and sweet. He was a cutie with his big green eyes and dark brown hair. Loma and I loved him immediately. Hatching up new plots with his best friend, Booey Hansen, kept him quite busy.

We hadn't been in Homer very long when Loma tripped over a root sticking up in the yard and got a nasty jagged cut on her knee. Lydia and I were trying to stop the bleeding and get her bandaged up when Sonny and Booey came into the house. Sonny patted Loma's shoulder saying, "Don't worry Sis, that thing will never hurt you again."

Upon closer investigation we found he had taken Daddy's good ax and chopped the root out at least six inches below the surface with such a vengeance the ground looked like it was ready for planting, and the blade of the ax — well, it was a little battle scarred.

From the slough we drove by Berry's store, later called the Inlet Trading Post, owned and operated by Maybell Berry. We bumped along the narrow gravel road and passed Bert Hansen's weathered log house on the left. Sonny pointed it out as his friend Booey's house. We continued on up the hill now called Main Street. A saw mill sat idle on the right. Daddy called it Garen Svedlund's mill. Guy Rosi's shop is there now. As we turned right at the corner we saw a large white building on the left.

"That's Auntie Walli's store," Sonny told us. "She calls it Homer Cash Store." Daddy shifted down, patted the dashboard, and said encouragingly, "Now come on Lena, climb the hill old girl." We made a left-hand turn up a steep little driveway toward a rather large story-and-a-half house with a natural shiplap exterior. When I looked at him questioningly about the dashboard patting Daddy smiled and explained, "The old truck's name is really 'Limpin' Lena but I call her Lena for short."

I laughed and patted the dashboard also, saying, "I am so glad to meet you, Lena. I hope we will be friends."

As I opened the truck door I was confronted by a very large gold-colored German shepherd-golden Lab dog. He studied me with his big brown eyes and I guess he decided I was acceptable since I was with Daddy and Sonny. I'm glad he liked me because I would find later he had very definite opinions about people. Daddy introduced us. "This is Tuffy. He was my lead dog when I was still using the dog team. Since the roads are better and we have 'Lena' he is retired." He gave Tuffy an affectionate pat on the head.

From that day forward Tuffy and I were best friends. I dared not step backward without checking for fear I would step on him. Of course, when Daddy was around I took second place.

The back door of the house opened and a wonderful aroma wafted out of the kitchen on the fresh spring air, reminding me how long it had been since I had eaten hot cakes and bacon at Juanita's place in Seldovia. Lydia stopped stirring the gravy that bubbled in the cast iron skillet atop the coal-fired range long enough to greet us.

She was small, only about five feet tall, with brown eyes and cap of short, dark, curly hair. I am sure she was nervous with two strange teen-agers moving into her house and life. Turning back to her gravy, she told Sonny to show us our room and then all come and eat.

The plywood walls of our room were painted soft pink. Sheer white curtains hung over the two windows at the end of the room that looked out over a yard filled with spruce trees and spindly leafless bushes. The bushes, in the warmer months that followed, were loaded with blueberries.

Our army cot beds were made up with warm woolly blankets and soft pillows and looked very inviting. A single electric bulb hung from the ceiling. Of course, I pulled the chain but nothing happened. I made a mental note to ask for a bulb as it must be burned out. There was a nail in the ceiling bent up into a hook. Now what was that for? I soon learned the hook was for a lamp that was fueled by Blazo gas to be used when the gas-powered generator wasn't on. I had never heard of this kind of electricity before but was pleasantly surprised when it came on and the whole house lit up.

The other half of the upstairs had shelves along the walls loaded with groceries like a store.

Back downstairs my first question was, "When can we go to see the town?"

"Young lady, you have just seen it," my dad answered firmly.

Although I was not a city girl, this was probably the least town I had ever seen in one place, so far from any place that was any place *and* no road to get there.

Lydia quickly tucked a slice of moose roast between two slices of homemade bread and Daddy took it with him back to help unload the scow. Sonny, with sandwich in hand, went with him. Lunch over, Lydia started the dishes, sending Loma and me off to organize our room.

Later that afternoon, Lydia answered a knock on the front door. Two young girls appeared in jeans and light jackets.

"Oh, I'm glad you came over," Lydia said. "Come meet the girls."

One of the visitors was the blondest natural blond I had ever seen, with very blue eyes. The other was a little taller with hazel eyes, golden brown hair and a wispy little smile.

The blond spoke first. "I am Sister Walli and this is my friend, Shirley Sholin."

I stood up and said, "Hi, I'm Wilma. This is my sister, Loma." Then cautiously I asked "Do you have a first name?" Somehow the thought of calling that beautiful girl Sister Walli didn't seem right.

"Yes, my name is Lillian," she answered, taking no offense at my rather blunt question.

"I'll call you Lil, if that is okay." I said, and in no time we were chatting amiably.

"We were wondering if you're going to the dance on Saturday night," Lil said.

"I don't know yet," I answered, wondering what the house rules were on that subject.

When Daddy returned from unloading the scow he paused to have a cup of coffee from the pot on the back of the coal stove, before he said, "Come on kids. We need to get you dressed for this country."

Obediently we followed him along the back trail. It led past the pump house, which had a tank on top. Sonny, anxious to help us get acquainted with our new surroundings, pointed to the tank and said, "That's where our running water comes from."

"We pump the water up into the tank with the hand pump then it is gravity flow to the house," Daddy added. "That building also holds the light plant that gives the lights for both our house and the store."

Arriving at the private rear entrance to the store, Daddy knocked and then opened the door saying, "Lilly, where are you?" She came into the kitchen from the adjoining store smiling.

"Oh Tom, the girls got here safe and sound."

Daddy introduced us, saying, "They sure did. Lilly, these are my girls, Wilma and Loma. Girls, this is Auntie Walli."

She was a large woman with a round face, blond hair in

a short perm, and wearing a print dress with an apron over it. I liked her friendly self-confident manner.

The Homer Cash Store had been built by Auntie and her husband Ero when they were still living at their fish trap at Stariski, 26 miles up the beach from Homer. They loved their Stariski home but wanted their children to be able to go to school. As fate would have it, Ero died shortly after the store was completed, leaving Auntie to run it and raise the children alone. In spite of her limited formal education she quickly learned the ropes and followed the plan that she and her husband had laid out.

The store was a large two-story building with high ceilings. Shelves lined the wall behind the counter. In the front right-hand corner was a small room with glass windows in the wall that separated it from the rest of the store. It held the liquor supplies. Several men were sitting in captains chairs around a big brown oil heater in the center of the store, chatting. On the opposite side of the store from the counter was a stack of case goods growing higher by the minute as a couple of young men unloaded a pickup full of supplies that had come over on the scow.

After greeting us warmly, Auntie sent us upstairs to the clothing department with Lil and Shirley to make our transition into Alaska attire. Daddy joined the group by the stove, while Sonny leaned on the arm of his chair soaking up the men's news of the day.

Selecting the clothes wasn't a complicated procedure as the selection was very limited. You had a choice of whether the flannel shirt would be red or blue. Whether the wool socks would be all gray or have red tops but the black shiny knee boots were all the same and in those days blue jeans were just that, blue jeans. No fancy cuts. In a small storage closet we changed into the new things then came out, slowly turning around seeking approval. The girls looked us over carefully.

Shirley said, "The shirttail has to come out."

"Roll the boot tops down one turn," Lil instructed.

We did and hurried downstairs to see how Daddy liked the "new" us. Auntie wrote the purchases down in a book. I didn't know exactly how the credit thing worked but at that time it seemed everyone bought a grocery order after fishing in the fall. From then on Homer Cash Store got very little cash until the next fishing season when everyone paid their bill and put in their winter order again.

The dance situation was solved that evening at the dinner table when Lydia said, "You girls need to decide what you are wearing to the dance tomorrow night."

My heart skipped a beat at the thought of going to a dance but there was one small problem. Very quietly I said, "I don't know how to dance."

Both Daddy and Lydia laughed.

"Don't worry. That won't last long," Lydia said.

Chapter 9

My First Homer Dance

The house bustled with activity Saturday afternoon. The oven in the coal-fired kitchen range sent forth a wonderful cinnamon aroma from the apple pies baking. Baked beans bubbled in a crockery pot. These things were for the midnight feast at the dance.

Loma and I searched our limited wardrobe, trying on one dress after another. What to wear for this momentous occasion? Soon our beds were piled with the no-not-thats and the not-just-rights. We decided to wash our hair and put it on pin curls. Time enough for the dresses later.

Lil and Shirley dropped by to check on us and see how we were doing in our preparations. We quickly enlisted their help in the dress decision-making. With their assistance it didn't take long, and our outfits were chosen, right down to the garter belt and silk stockings. Loma had settled on a light blue pan satin with a sweetheart neck. I would wear the light green with the lace collar and pearl buttons. Both had the full swing skirts so popular at the time. I set out my cream-colored high heels but Loma, being self-conscious about her height, stuck with the Cuban heels.

The afternoon passed slowly. With dinner and dishes over, at long last it was time! We dressed, checked our stocking seams to see that they were straight, and I gave my long pageboy hairdo a last smoothing gesture. Loma's curls were brushed into place and, taking a deep breath, we walked slowly down the stairs.

Our five-year-old brother gave us the confidence we needed when he said in an awed voice, "Gosh, you guys are beautiful."

Wasn't God just wonderful when he sent little brothers? We did realize that his opinion might be biased, but we loved his attitude.

Our transportation was, of course, "Limpin' Lena" with her one seat dressed for the evening with a soft pink blanket. Lena was not really built to take the whole family to the dance but we managed nicely since it was only half a mile. Daddy drove, looking great in his dark blue suit, white shirt and tie. Lydia sat next to him looking beautiful. Her unruly dark curls bobbed with the motion of the truck. She held Sonny on her lap and I held Loma.

I was excited but a little apprehensive. Loma ducked her head to keep it from hitting the top of the cab as we joggled over a bumpy spot in the road.

Lydia said "Drive careful, Tom, so you don't spill the baked beans."

I stole a quick look out the back window of the truck to see if the beans and pie box sitting in the bed of the truck, was still upright in spite of the jostling. So far, so good.

Daddy pulled up and parked as near as possible to the back door of the Women's Club Hall. Light shone out of the window, spilling out across the snow-covered road. Three slippery steps led up to the main entrance of the 30-by-30 unpainted plywood building. The walls inside were covered with plywood, creamy colored in its newness. There was no ceiling. An electric wire wound around one of the rafters ended with a single 100 watt light bulb that flickered a bit as the little light plant putted away conscientiously out behind the building. I had never in my 15 years of life seen a public building quite like this but it worked *great*.

The building had been built by the Homer Women's Club to hold their meetings in. It had taken a lot of box socials at the school to raise the funds to buy the materials for the building and a lot of sweet talk to get the husbands to build it. Never underestimate the power of a determined woman, and this was a whole group of them. One of the factors that had promoted the original idea of a building was that as civilization and progress seeped into the community the Department of Education voiced objection to community activities taking place in the school as it was considered state's property.

Five or six families were already at the hall when we arrived. A few were from the village proper but the majority had come miles from their homesteads. A lady walked by me with a box of Ivory soap flakes, sprinkling it generously over the floor. I looked at her curiously, trying to figure out why on earth she was putting soap on the floor.

"That makes the floor slick and easier to dance on," my dad explained, seeing my curious glance. "Works great except where people track in snow by the door. It gets pretty slick." He laughed.

Daddy was talking to someone and I stood listening to the bits of conversation that were strange to me: "We got our patent papers this week. It sure has been a long haul proving up." What in the world are they talking about? "Glad to hear it. I still have to clear another five acres before I can apply for mine. I am afraid it will be another year." That is a long time to be proving something. From another area: "Are you still interested in the bear paw snowshoes that I showed you?" How in the world did that poor bear get tangled up with the snowshoes? "Can you give me a hand with the telephone line tomorrow? It is still working but it needs to be worked on where it is coming loose from the trees." Strange talk to these young Cheechako ears.

The wall over in one corner was covered with coats hanging on nails. That was fine, but what on earth were all of those packboards doing sitting on the floor beneath them? Why would anyone take a packboard to a dance?

The food was whisked away to the warm oven in the oil-fired range in the lean-to kitchen. Women took turns checking their hairdos and lipstick in the small mirror on the wall in the kitchen. I wondered, "Why don't they use the mirror in the bathroom, wherever that might be."

Then one of the ladies said, "Anyone want to go on this expedition to the little girl's room before I turn the gas lantern out? Grab a roll of paper off of the shelf there. I think all that's out there is what's left of a very old, very cold Sears catalog." Four of the ladies pulled on their coats and followed her down the narrow shoveled-out pathway toward a small outbuilding.

53

I drifted back into the main hall just as an elderly couple came in the main entrance. The man stood over six feet tall with a shock of silver hair and laughing blue eyes. One long arm was wrapped around a rather battered violin case. The very petite lady with him had her gray hair pulled back quite severely into a bun at the nape of her neck. Her kindly face broke into a warm smile as people came to greet her. She progressed toward the piano in the far corner and laid a packet of sheet music on the bench while she pulled off her overshoes and heavy knitted gloves.

"Pa! Are you and Ma playing tonight?" someone called out.

The answer came back with a strong Norwegian accent. "Ya shure. You betcha." He waved his violin case.

Daddy took Loma and me on an introduction tour around the hall, introducing us to everyone. I tried hard to remember names but there were just so many new people.

Children dressed in their best played near their parents. The women wore bright-colored dresses and high heels. The men were either in suits or blue jeans and white shirts, but the most beautiful thing was the aura of friendliness and warmth that was everywhere.

Ma, now sitting at the upright piano, struck a chord and Pa turned from his conversation with a friend and placed the violin beneath his chin. He pulled the bow across the strings. Music burst forth in the rousing strains of the old schottische "From 'Frisco to Cape Cod." Soon the floor was alive with stomping and swinging.

I was asked to dance. The wonderful moment I had waited for. I looked up at the gentleman then out at the dancers on the dance floor. My terrified body wouldn't move. I couldn't do that! I declined saying, "Please ask me again later; this is the first time I have even seen this dance done."

I wanted to become invisible. I couldn't dance and share in the fun everyone was having. I looked out at the sea of dancers and saw my braver-than-I sister dancing and doing quite well. My folks were dancing. Even my little brother was handling the intricate steps like he had done them every day of his life. He was swinging a little girl around and around, never missing a beat.

Jim and Marion Waddell waltzed with their three-year-old, Gail, perched on their entwined arms. Little Mac Cambell slept peacefully on the bench, his head resting on his mother's folded coat, covered with his dad's parka. His parents, Scotty and Ann, danced nearby, keeping a watchful eye on him. They had hiked the six miles down from their homestead on Diamond Ridge, carrying Mac in a packboard, to take a break from homesteading life and enjoy their friends.

In the musical corner, Pa stamped his foot to the music as he dragged the bow across the strings of his violin with gusto. His eyes sparkled and I saw him wink at Ma, who was looking up at him with adoration. Lydia floated like a feather in Daddy's arms as they danced around the floor.

As the evening progressed with polkas and rye waltzes I hung back, not wanting to start my life in Homer by falling down on the dance floor or stepping on somebody's feet. I looked up to see my father whispering to Ma and Pa, who smiled and nodded. Then to the strains of the "Blue Skirt Waltz" my dad coaxed me onto the dance floor. My heart pounded in fear during those first steps but Daddy was a strong leader and very patient. I survived and never sat down again all evening.

I noticed the men going outside in twos and threes. Quite often, I might add. Why were they venturing out into that crisp March weather? I asked my dad.

"Well, you see, they have their bottles tucked away under the edge of the building. They bring things like homebrew, homemade elderberry wine and home canned raspberry juice spiked with a little gin. You know, homesteading isn't easy and this is their way of relaxing a bit."

I was still a little nervous about people drinking but no one was doing anything more than swinging the girls around with a little extra enthusiasm, and Lawrence hadn't attacked us with his ax. Daddy didn't seem worried, so I decided not to worry either.

About midnight, the women started going into the kitchen. When the serving window from the kitchen opened, the wonderful aroma of good things to eat filled the hall. Soon we were filling our plates with baked beans, potato salad, scalloped potatoes and perog, which is Russian fish pie. There were bowls of pickled salmon, and quart Mason jars of deep red pickled beets harvested from those homestead gardens the summer before. It seemed that every housewife had made something wonderful to make the evening

55

special. Come to think of it, some of those old bachelors cooked up some outstanding dishes too, but mostly they brought smoked fish or moose jerky because it was easy to carry on the packboard.

When everyone finished eating, I noticed a young woman wearing her dancing dress and high heels pick up one of the packboards and vanish into the kitchen. Soon several others followed. The men talked while they pulled off their polished oxfords, replacing them with shoepacs pulled from beneath the bench.

When the women returned they looked very different. Shoepacs had replaced the delicate high-heeled shoes. The hair that had been piled high on top of the head now hung in long braids that were soon tucked beneath a parka hood. Snow pants and fur mittens completed their truly Alaskan outfits. They looked as though they could handle a blizzard competently.

Packing to leave, they wrapped their now empty food bowls in dish towels. These were then tucked into the packboard along with mail, Sears packages and groceries picked up earlier. Sleepy children were tucked into their dads' packboards, bundled in snowsuits and mittens, their woolly caps pulled down securely on their nodding heads. One by one the gas lanterns were lit for lighting their way home.

"We left the skis up where the snow starts getting deep," one young man said, "so we'll make it to the cabin fine. We did see quite a few moose signs but no moose on the way down. I hope we don't see one going home. I'd sure hate to see the wife try to make it up a tree with her skis on."

Everyone laughed. One of the fellows said, "I'm going to give you a lift as far as I can make it with the truck. I'm chained up so I should be able to make it quite a ways. It'll take the edge off of the trip home carrying the little guy."

"Hey buddy, that's the best news I've heard lately. Right, Mama?"

"Oh yes!" said the lady near him, shouldering into her packboard.

With that, the homesteader picked up his sleeping son and with many "see you laters," followed the volunteer driver into the cold moonlit night. Others followed, their lanterns making little swinging patches of light on the packed snow as they hurried homeward.

My father motioned us toward the door with a wave of his hand. My little brother, who incidentally had never slowed down, was carrying the pie plate for his mother. I was a little suspicious that the one piece of pie left in the pan might have a bearing on his willingness to tote and carry.

Lil and Shirley were riding home with us, so Loma and I opted to ride in the back of the truck with them. We all made ourselves comfortable sitting on the wooden gas cases as the truck bumped along and we sang songs we had heard at the dance such as "I'll Walk Alone" and "Mexacali Rose."

As Daddy shifted into second gear to take us up the hill I looked back. The full moon made a soft yellow path across the icy waters of Kachemak Bay. The mountains across the bay glistened in their snow crusted glory. I couldn't help but smile. What a wonderful evening.

Chapter 10

Learning the Steps

My first real dancing instructions came when Lil's brother Bob came home from deck-handing on the *Monterey* for Jack Anderson. When he went to the first dance after his return home we danced several times. The following morning when I went into the store he said something subtle to me like, "We simply have to do something about your dancing."

"That bad, huh?" And the lessons began. After store hours it was up and down the aisles of the Homer Cash store with Lil and Loma changing the records on the record player. The schottisches and polkas were in our kitchen because we had linoleum tiles that were just right to 1-2-3 hop, 1-2-3 swing. Daddy and Lydia took all of this hopping and noise in stride.

Two weeks after our arrival in Homer the next *Cordova* came in. The ice-damaged dock had been repaired so the boat was able to land at Homer this time. Everyone in town was on hand for this major event: the arrival of the steamer. Some came out of curiosity, some to pick up freight or incoming passengers. We were there, you bet; it was the most exciting thing that happened in those days.

Beebe and Vada Gray were there with their two little girls, Ethyl Jean and Carolyn, and Beebe's brother, Glenn. They were there to meet Vada's family, the Maxwells, who were coming in from El Paso, Texas. When she saw them coming down the gangplank she ran to meet them. I couldn't possibly have imagined that day what role Vada's brother Lloyd would play in my life.

Lil and I had ridden out with Milo, who worked at her mother's store. Milo loaded the fresh produce quickly and we went back to town. It was not until the next day, when they came to the store and post office, that we saw the Maxwell family up close. Lloyd, Carlene and Dorothy were about our ages. They had a real southern drawl and we were a little surprised to hear a paper bag called a poke.

Lloyd had already graduated from high school, but the girls hiked the four miles from what is now Skyline Drive to school in Homer. When the weather was nice this wasn't a problem, but on bad days Lloyd picked them up and took them as far as he could drive, which took a couple of miles off of their hike home.

The following year, the Maxwells took up a homestead on the side hill and their older son Harreld came home to help cut and haul the logs for the house. The whole family pitched in to get the house built. When it was finished, true to the homestead methods of the times, Lloyd and Harreld carried household items that were ordered from Sears up the hillside path on their backs. Lloyd melded into our little bunch of teenagers, going to the dances, playing ball on the front beach and whatever other things we were doing.

There were so many firsts for me that year that it is hard to find a place to start. First of all, Lydia was the Homer postmaster and our house was also the post office. I had never lived with a post office before but found it very interesting.

Jack Anderson had the mail contract on the inlet with his two boats, the *Princess Pat* and the *Monterey*. He ran the *Monterey* and his son Junior ran the *Pat*. They started from Anchorage, stopping at Kenai, Kasilof, Ninilchik, Homer, Seldovia, Iliamna and then back to Anchorage.

When mail arrived by boat or plane, Bill Putnam, who had the local mail contract, would bring the pouches to the post office and unload them. There was always a flurry of excitement as this was not a daily thing but a whenever-they-got-here thing. It had to be sorted into the A, B, C designated compartments. Everyone picked up their mail at the window like general delivery. Since there were only about 150 people from the head of Kachemak Bay to Anchor Point, that didn't create a problem. I felt very important when I was allowed to help sort the mail and answer the window, and it helped Lydia.

When that task was completed I would grab Walli's mail and deliver it to the store. That was appreciated until the first bank of real store-bought mailboxes were installed. Then Lil wanted me to call her and tell her it was sorted so she could come in to the front part of the post office and open her own mail box.

I got acquainted quickly and soon knew everybody. I even learned the names and sounds of all of the cars in town. Hugh Watson's old pickup truck, without a muffler, was "Rosie," Stanley Nielson drove a bright blue T-model Ford called "Blue Bird" — incidentally, he had learned to drive in Homer and might pass you on either side, coming or going. Auntie Walli's Ford pickup was "Wheezie Eight" and so on.

People who had walked the sixteen miles down the beach from Anchor Point or the five or six miles off the hill were often invited to lunch while they waited for the mail to get in. They showed their appreciation by bringing Lydia things from their gardens, smoked fish, or jams and jellies they had made.

Jens Jensen brought her the first crab apples from his tree. It was the first tree of that type in the area and he was very proud. There are very few fruit trees of any kind in the Homer area.

Loma went to school in an old log cabin on the banks of Woodard Creek about a mile from our house. The teachers, Lyman and Margaret Allen, lived across the street in the old Woodard house with their two little boys. I didn't go back to school as they were not teaching any of the subjects that I had been taking in Oregon and it was too late in the year to hope to catch up on entirely new ones. The Allens needed a baby-sitter and I got the job caring for their two little boys. It gave me something to do and I could usually walk home with Loma.

The particular type of telephone used locally was a new experience. The beach had one line and the hill another. You reached your party by cranking the phone a long and a short ring or whatever their combination of longs and shorts might be. To call someone on the hill line you called Auntie Walli, three shorts, at the store. She had two phones and would ring the right amount of longs and shorts for your party on the hill phone. When they answered she would throw the switch between the phones and tell you to go ahead. Great to have this service, providing it was not a very personal matter, since, as there was little excitement in those days and for lack of something better to do, the whole town picked up their receivers when the phone rang.

At times maintenance of the phone line got a little complicated. It was supposed to be a community affair but the ones toward the end of the line, to whom it was most important, seemed to end up doing the main part of the repairs. At a town meeting this matter came to a head between two of the men. There was a brief intermission while we all went outdoors and they proceeded to settle it with their fists. Once this was resolved, the meeting resumed. There was no financial cost, they didn't have to wait for a court date, and the results were great. You would be surprised how eager the slacker was to do his share.

One call we all waited for was Buddug Waddell ringing a general alarm on the phone from her home on the side hill to announce in her very Welsh accent, "The *Cordova* is coming around Seldovia Point and heading for Homer."

Oh the excitement! After I had been there awhile Auntie would let Lil and me drive her Ford pickup to the dock to pick up the fresh produce from the boat. We tried to arrive as the gangplank was put in place, checking to see who the new arrivals were. Then we would go aboard to play the one-armed bandit, buy funny books and maybe a movie magazine from the little ship's store. We kept an eye on the unloading crew, checking every few minutes to see if the sling loads of fresh produce were being unloaded yet. When that happened, we would hurry ashore to load the pickup.

Back at the store a crowd gathered, anxiously awaiting our arrival. Well, not us exactly, but our cargo. As we pulled up to the side door, eager hands would help with the unloading. At first it seemed silly for people to be so excited about apples, oranges, fresh meat and salad things, but before many weeks I understood. People hadn't had these things since shortly after the last boat. The boxes literally flowed from the back of the truck to the counter where they were quickly opened. Milo, Auntie, Bob and Lil were all kept busy accepting money, weighing things and writing in the little credit books.

Auntie had a small freezer that helped preserve the meat, but it was not the total answer as the light plant usually ran only when it was needed for lights. This left the freezer without power for hours each day.

In the next few days the rest of the freight had to be hauled from the warehouse on the end of the dock. Occasionally Lil and I were allowed to take the big truck, a two-and-a-half ton Chevrolet. This was a special honor for which we were willing to work like little slaves. The case goods were a snap, but the flour and sugar came in hundred-pound sacks and took a little more imagination. We would drag the sacks to the back of the truck, grab two corners each, lift, swing and push. It's a wonder we didn't have muscles like Atlas.

If the tides were big, the water covered the road at the end of the Spit toward the mainland. Four-wheel drives were still a thing of the future, so a person must drive well or carry a jack and a lot of planks. It helped to catch it just after the tide had subsided and while the sand was compact, be sure to be in a low enough gear so you didn't have to shift, pour on the coal and keep rolling. I hate to jack up trucks, so I became quite proficient.

The road across the slough, which is now Beluga Lake, was not much of a road either. It also suffered from tidal action, leaving deep ruts if used when it was soft. Keep moving and avoid ruts as much as possible were the rules. If you high-centered you were in trouble. I don't remember ever getting stuck, but I do remember being scared to death I was going to.

When my children ask me, "Weren't you bored without a movie or anything to do?" my answer has always been, "Never, ever." Homer was a most wonderful place to grow up. With our busy little minds thinking up things to do, there was never a dull moment.

Often six or eight of us would take the .22 caliber rifles and hike up the beach to Bluff Point nine miles away, taking a lunch along. After eating our picnic lunch we would hike back, have dinner and go the dance.

Along the way we visited the old bachelors, Jens Jensen and Dick Gray. They were glad for the company and we loved to hear their stories. Dick Gray's place was six miles up the beach and on top of the bluff near Diamond Creek. There were steep steps to climb up the 200 foot bluff. He had installed a double block pulley system to bring up his coal and groceries that worked well. Dick was well educated and his cabin walls

63

were lined with books. On our visits we sipped hot black tea and ate crackers while he told us stories.

Jens served us cool, delicious home-canned raspberries he brought from his cellar. He would laugh about having a limited amount of dishes. We didn't mind we had to share, two to a dish.

I hadn't been in Homer long before I got my first lesson in beach driving. I drove the truck down to the slough, where the men were working on their boats, to pick Daddy up. I made a wide swing to turn around near the slough entrance. With my limited experience with loose beach gravel, I got on the downhill side and spun the wheels. I cramped the wheels harder up the beach as I eyed the incoming tide. Things went from bad to worse. The more I tried to get up the beach, the further I slid toward the water. I was panic-stricken and it didn't help that the men were sitting on their boat decks sipping coffee and watching. I hated to ask for help. I wanted desperately to solve my own problem. The tide edged ever nearer to the area I was frantically plowing up with the back tires.

I was so afraid my dad would holler at me and say I couldn't take the truck again. Maybe he wouldn't even like me anymore. How awful, and just when I was getting to know him again. My worries had gained momentous proportions when I noticed he and several other men were coming toward me. I was scared and ready to cry when he said in a kindly voice, "Here, let me give you a hand. You know I have been at this a lot longer than you have."

He gave me a little hug, slid into the driver's seat, turned the wheels down toward the water, and with a little pushing encouragement from the others, drove it out of the predicament I had gotten into.

It was a lesson about beach driving, and about my dad too. I had followed him everywhere as a small child and we were resuming a good relationship. Don't think that he never got upset with me, or that I was never defiant. I was fifteen. Remember that is the age when you know everything and nothing works quite right.

That experience was only the beginning of my beach adventures. Another one really stands out in my mind. The two firm rules where the truck was concerned were: You take it, you bring it back, and you do something worthwhile with it, such as bring coal for the stove or gravel for the driveway. I have a very personal interest in Shelford Street in Homer from the many loads of gravel I contributed. I did so love to drive that truck.

I was alone, headed down the beach toward Homer with a load of coal. I stopped to throw on another piece of coal but when I went to put the truck in gear it wouldn't move. The gear shift felt funny. The engine sounded fine, but I wasn't going anywhere. I looked at the incoming tide, then my watch. That tide was coming in fast and I had the family transportation in harm's way. Bad combination.

I tried to think what to do. There just wouldn't be time for me to get help. What would make it stop when the engine was okay? It must be the transmission. I took up the floor board. No big deal on a Model A. I got out the little tool box that Daddy always kept in the truck. The top wasn't too hard to get off of the transmission. Ah-ha! The shifting fork was broken.

The rippling waters of Kachemak Bay made little splashing noises on the rocks twenty feet away. No time to fizzle out. Nothing ventured, nothing gained. I looked over the meager assortment of tools and got out the big screw driver, started up the truck, put in the clutch. With the screw driver, somehow I managed to get it into a gear that took me chugging happily up to the high, high beach away from the menacing tide, in case of further difficulty, and then home.

When I got home Daddy was reading the paper.

"Hi," I said rather cautiously.

He smiled and said, "How did things go?"

"I got a load of coal." Give him the good news first, now the follow up. "And, well, I had a little problem that I wanted to talk to you about. I think the shifting fork is broken in Lena's transmission."

I thought he paled a little.

"Where is the truck?"

"It's here in the yard, but it quit shifting down on the beach. I had to shift with a screwdriver to get home."

I definitely had his undivided attention now. He laid down the paper. His nervousness may have stemmed from the fact I had shown some mechanical interest in the gasoline washing machine earlier, with rather poor results.

"Let's go take a look."

He smiled as he looked at the transmission. All he said was, "Get a cloth to put around it to keep the dirt out till I can fix it." Whew! Was I glad that adventure had a happy ending.

I did upset Daddy sometimes, like when I decided to target practice. I had never been around guns before coming to Alaska. My friend Lil was a pretty good shot. I thought maybe if I practiced I would be, too. Everyone was busy and Daddy's rifles were sitting in a little closet in the kitchen.

I decided it would be a good time to practice. I chose a 30-40 Krag. I didn't know the name of it then, but I liked the stock and it looked like a good sturdy gun. Now for a target. It didn't seem like a good idea to shoot at a full gas drum because the gas might leak out of the holes if I got lucky and hit it. But why not an empty? Backing off, I drew a bead on the middle of the empty drum. Now there is no doubt that I hit it, as the sound of the explosion was deafening. I do not know where my dad was, but anyone this side of Seldovia would have heard it. The kick from the big rifle knocked me back against the porch wall and set me to thinking this may not have been one of my best ideas.

When Daddy arrived on the run, there was a brief conversation that ended my association with any heavy artillery. Oh well, I do better with a camera anyway.

A favorite pastime was playing cards. Lil taught me to play two-handed pinochle and penny-ante poker. Winter afternoons would find us sitting around Auntie's round oak kitchen table involved in a serious game of poker. Of course our bank roll was a pound of navy beans. We didn't go as far as the green visors but there was great deliberation before making the bet of two small white beans, with great moaning and groaning if we lost. After the game the beans went back into the coffee can for the next game. Auntie was aware they were not for human consumption.

Making root beer was a fun project. When it was bottled we took it upstairs and set it by the stove pipe. This went quite well until we either put too much yeast in, or left it too long by the stovepipe. The bad part was that Lydia was having a Homemakers meeting in the living room when the bottles started exploding. It was a very disruptive situation as the root beer made a real sonic BOOM and then the contents ran down the stovepipe into the living room below where the meeting was in progress. Needless to say, we were busy girls cleaning up that sticky mess of root beer and broken glass. Facing Lydia's wrath at having her meeting disrupted was the worst of all.

That spring of 1941, we decided to take a 26-mile hike up the beach to see Lil's old home at Stariski. We planned carefully. There would be four of us girls going: Phoebe James, Loma, Lil and I. I was 15, Lil and Phoebe were 14 and Loma was 12. The main menu must be lightweight because we would have to carry it 26 miles. Weighing each item, we divided it up into four 35-pound packs.

All supplies were put in bags and tied securely to our packboards the night before we were to leave. Glenn Gray and Lloyd Maxwell had offered to drive us to the end of the road and walk part of the way with us. The day of departure dawned bright and clear. Auntie's upstairs looked like a girls' dormitory. I hope we didn't keep her awake with our giggling most of the night. However, when the boys came by to pick us up at 4:30 a.m. we were up and ready.

The early hour was to take full advantage of the outgoing tide in the area where tide and bluff meet. The boys drove us to Bidarka Creek. We walked through Gordon's field and slid down the old trail past Rose's cabin. (I think that the beach has eroded and long since taken the cabin away.) The boys walked with us just beyond Diamond Creek.

In Homer, where there are few secrets, we learned later that Lil's mother and my father didn't rest until they saw the boys back in town. Adults always have such suspicious minds. Time was of the essence and we moved right along in order to make the crossing at Anchor River at low tide.

At Troublesome Creek a man with a white beard and wearing a battered hat was working a sluice box. I had only been here two months and I was excited about the prospects of meeting a real live "sourdough." He really looked the part. As we walked to high beach where he was working, he saw us coming, and stood, taking off his hat. Then he spoke in a very cultured voice, saying, "Good Morning ladies. How nice to have company. May I fix you a cup of tea?"

We declined, saying we had to make Anchor River at low water and could only stop a few minutes. He showed us how the sluice worked and in the course of the conversation told us he was a retired college professor.

"I like what I am doing here," he said, "sluicing out a little gold and trapping coyotes for the bounty. My income is about the same as it was being a professor." He smiled, "with a lot less politics." He sat down on a rock to rest and was still watching us when we reached low beach, turned and waved good-bye. We hurried along on the hard sand at low beach, very conscious of the fact we would have to sleep on the beach with the wandering wildlife if we missed our fording time.

We hurried along so well that we reached Anchor River early, giving us time to stop and visit Al Lofgren. The tantalizing aroma of fresh bread came from his cabin as he opened the door. He offered us fresh coffee and a couple of slices each of that wonderful homemade bread. I never drink coffee; but I did that day. We were starved after that 20-mile hike.

He proudly took us on a tour of his garden with its giant-size vegetables. I couldn't resist asking him what he used for fertilizer.

"Well," he explained, "we have the best fertilizer around right here at our front door. I get kelp off of the beach, wash the salt out by putting it in a rack in the river." I was fascinated. He took great pleasure in telling us about his garden. It was surrounded by a five-foot-high, alder pole and chicken wire fence to keep the moose out.

At slack water we thanked him for the wonderful lunch and got our packs on. He walked with us to the river and watched while we made the crossing. It was too deep to wear our knee boots without the water going over the tops. We pulled them off and stuffed them into our packboards, crossing in bare feet. Al laughed good naturedly at our howls as we stuck our feet into that icy water. I swear that river comes straight from the North Pole. Once across, we rubbed our feet vigorously to get them thawed out before putting our boots back on. Waving good-bye to Al across the river, we started up the last stretch of our journey.

Those last six miles seemed like we were on a treadmill. Stariski lay in the distance, and no matter how fast we walked it seemed we were not gaining. Finally, we walked up to high beach, crossed Stariski River on the piling bridge and up the little hill to that beautiful old log cabin. Just a little over nine hours walking time. I want you to know we were very tired girls.

Rickard, Auntie's caretaker, welcomed us and brought over a fresh rhubarb pie. I think I did something real ingenious that evening for dinner like open a couple of cans of pork and beans and slice a loaf of bread. Topped off with the flaky-crusted pie we were in good shape. We played cards by the light of the kerosene lamp and crawled into our sleeping bags early. No giggling that night.

The following morning, I washed the pie tin and took it back to Rickard.

"We really enjoyed that pie. I don't think I have ever seen such flaky crust. What kind of shortening did you use?" I asked.

"Oh, I was lucky this year and got an early black bear, so I have plenty of good bear grease for baking and, of course, for treating my shoes to keep them water repellent." I sincerely hope my expression didn't change. Being new to the country I was still pretty much Cheechako. The idea of eating bear grease took some getting used to.

On the fifth day we were to return home. We got up early and packed. Lil had a bad headache and didn't feel well at all. By the time we were a mile down the beach it became obvious she had no business trying to make the hike to Homer that day. Time for a conference. The decision was that Loma and Phoebe should go on home to keep the folks from worrying. I would go back to Stariski with Lil and we would come down the next day if she felt better. If we didn't show in two days' time they were to ask Daddy to pick us up with the boat, as it would mean Lil was still sick.

We felt very proud of our planning until we started to get hungry and discovered that we had sent all of the groceries home with the girls and we had only our rifles and several sleeping bags. Our food supply was half a box of Cream of Wheat we had left in the cabin.

Lil took a couple of aspirins and curled up on the bed. In a couple of hours she woke up feeling better and we discussed the food situation.

"There are king salmon in the river," Lil said.

I laughed.

"I think we would have a heck of a time getting one with a .22. We don't have any fishing tackle."

Lil sat up, looking thoughtful.

"Let's walk down to the mouth of the river. That .22 thing may not be as crazy as it sounds."

Filling the clips on our rifles and putting extra shells in our pockets we headed toward the mouth of the river. On the river bank, we lay on our tummies watching the fish coming in flipping and jumping in the crystal clear water.

"I wonder if we put some rocks across the river so the fish had to go over them if it would help?" I suggested.

"Let's try it," Lil agreed.

With the rocks in place we perched ourselves on the bank with our rifles aimed at the makeshift obstruction. Several futile potshots had been fired when a huge king attempted the crossing.

"Now!" Lil shouted.

We unloosed a volley of shots at what we hoped would be our dinner. I am sure anyone within miles would have thought there was a major enemy invasion going on. We managed a couple of good head shots before we threw down the rifles and jumped in the river after the fish. Somehow, we got a firm hold in the gills and dragged him ashore where we all, fish, Lil and I, lay gasping for breath. It helped our perseverance a lot to have not eaten since early morning. Now how were we going to get this 40-pound fish to the house? Good question. Finding a big stick we stuck it through its gills. Then with a "one, two, three" lift, we lifted it till the ends of the stick rested on each of our shoulders and headed to the cabin. Wonderful salmon steak for dinner. Next morning we headed for Homer with wonderful memories. Some years later I wrote the following amateur attempt at poetry:

STARISKI

Away up Cook Inlet,
A few miles above Kachemak Bay,
There's a lovely green valley,
That holds memories bright and gay.

There is only a house and a river
The Inlet and a clear blue sky
A lot of beach to walk on
And a few fish swimming by.

But there is a peace and quiet
So restful, tranquil and free,
Truly a balm to the troubled heart
Such wonderful memories for me.

   You can tell that I am not related to Longfellow but the thought is there anyhow.

Chapter 11

Becoming an Independent Person

In early June of 1941, when we got back from Stariski, I started making plans for the summer. I wrote Snug Harbor Packing Co. and asked Eric Friebrock, the owner, for a job. I was accepted. There was a $300 guarantee, plus room, board, transportation and overtime. I was delighted. I had never had $300 of my own in my whole 15 years of life.

On June 15th the message came on the shortwave radio that Snug Harbor's tender *Orient* would pick up the fifteen crew members on the 20th at the Homer dock. It was my very first adventure out into the world; I could hardly wait.

On the 20th I was up, had my duffel packed and sleeping bag rolled by 7 a.m., though the boat wasn't due till 10 a.m.. No sense in being late. Daddy drove me to the boat in "Limpin' Lena," down the bumpy, gravel road. On the Spit, horses grazed on the lush spring grass, barely raising their heads as we chugged by at a rousing 35 mph. Loma and Lil rode along to give me a good send off. As we drove out to the Spit we could see the *Orient* off Yukon Island, plowing steadily toward the dock.

We waited at the watchman's cabin, talking to Charlie Erickson, the dock man. Charlie's cabin, Daddy's old gear shed — later to become the Salty Dawg Saloon — and a small warehouse on the dock were the only buildings on the Spit in 1941.

Ing Narlin brought the 70-foot *Orient* dockside where we were waiting. One of the deck hands came up on the dock and let our gear down with a hand line. People soon made a human chain down the long ladder boarding the boat.

The boat had arrived close to low water in order to catch a fair tide back up the Inlet to Snug Harbor. Practical idea for travel, but with my fear of heights it looked like an awful long ways down to that boat. I, the great adventuress going forth into the world for the first time, must not allow myself the luxury of disintegrating into a quivering mass on the first leg of my journey, even if I was scared to death. That thought is what got me down the ladder that day.

Trying to look very self-confident, clamping my jaws together firmly to keep my teeth from chattering, I went over the edge of the dock and started down the ladder. I went past the gray weathered rungs, past the rungs covered with barnacles, and on past the ones slimy kelp clung to. Finally I felt that wonderful "bull rail" of the *Orient* under my feet.

I happened to look toward the upper boat deck. Ing stood there watching me, grinning as though he saw right through my calm exterior to my quivering insides. I busied myself taking pictures of Loma and Lil as they peeked over the dock, waving. In minutes the lines were loosed and we were underway. As I stood on the aft deck, watching Homer fade into the distance, I tried to analyze the sadness that came over me.

"Come on, Wilma," I said to myself, "You know you said you wouldn't stay in Homer. Soon you'll go back to the 'states' and forget Alaska." But somehow it didn't ring true.

Everybody laughed and talked the first hour aboard, as we made our way out of Kachemak Bay toward Cook Inlet. I went topside and was even allowed to steer the boat. One nice thing about a boat is, nobody has to worry about you running into a ditch.

Off Anchor Point, we started getting some weather. It didn't take long for all conversation and laughter to stop.

I will never forget poor John Dudas sitting on a gear box on the aft deck topside. Some thoughtful deck hand had lashed John there with a big line so he wouldn't fall overboard but he still begged each passerby in his Danish accent: "Tro me offerboard. I vant to die."

We were all feeling some distress. Ing offered Pat Myhill and me his bunk in the wheelhouse which helped immensely, although we did take a few urgent trips to the rail. Needless to say, the westerly side of Cook Inlet with the sheltered waters of Tuxedni Bay were a welcome sight. The high bluffs of

Chisik Island were alive with gulls. Every nook and cranny on that 200-foot sheer bluff had a gull's nest on it. I tried later to take pictures there, but the sea gulls had a rather liquid form of registering their displeasure at my intrusion so I gave up the idea. It took awhile to get the lens of the camera clean enough to take pictures again anyway.

At the cannery, a supervisor assigned the crew rooms. Mine had a window overlooking the bay, which I dearly loved. Sometimes, when I need to think of something tranquil to settle my ruffled nerves, I picture the view from that window. The blue-green waters of Tuxedni Bay bathed in sunshine, with the musical background supplied by the gulls, the steep rocky bluffs soaring to the blue sky across the bay making the picture complete.

My roommate, Pat Myhill, was married, but her husband didn't come over that first year. She was an ambitious person with a great sense of humor that helped to make it a fun summer.

We all waited for the mail as if our lives depended on it. Loma and Lil were good about writing. I got letters now and then from Gram, but I was still punishing her for sending me into exile in Alaska. Who knows how a teen-ager's mind works? Even when I knew that Alaska was the greatest thing that had ever happened to me, I still made little barbed remarks until I grew up a little and accepted life as it is. Gram did not deserve such treatment, and over the years I have deeply regretted my actions.

At Snug Harbor the cannery workers were allowed a lot of freedom in the off hours but there were rules. The boys could visit, if they liked, but not in our room. We could play cards or visit in the large hallway that was a thoroughfare to all of the rooms.

The Filipino cannery workers were generous about sharing their volleyball court. We had to have a cannery foreman go with us if we played, as young ladies didn't go unsupervised much then. In later years, when Loma and Lil were there, we were invited to dinner at the Filipino mess hall. The meal was wonderful and served with great care. Musicians played music of the islands while we ate. Their instruments were often improvised. The base fiddle was a wash tub with a broom handle inserted snugly into its upturned bottom. A string was tied from the edge of the tub to the upper end of the broom handle. The handle was moved around to create different tones. The lovely gentle songs of the early '40s lent themselves nicely to their style: "As Time Goes By," "I'll Walk Alone" — and I never hear "Aloha" without seeing the Filipino musicians in my mind standing there on the beach playing as we pulled out for Homer that fall.

The Filipino crew had one alarming habit that was unnerving at first. When they were working long hours, in the butchering area, they would suddenly wave their knives over their heads and holler at the top of their voices. It was a relaxation thing for them and, once I understood it was not some sort of uprising, I took it in stride.

I asked one day if they had electricity in Manila. They looked at me carefully to see if I was just ignorant or if I was being insulting. They enlightened me quickly that Manila is a very modern city.

There wasn't a lot to do for recreation, but I was allowed to go aboard the tenders to play penny-ante poker with the crew. I carried my entire bankroll of pennies and nickels to the boat in a pint jar.

The dining arrangement took a little getting used to. Everyone would gather in front of the mess hall about ten minutes before the cook rang the dinner bell. When the door opened, we all trooped in and sat on the benches stretching along tables about 30 feet long. Every 10 feet there was a family-size set up of dishes holding about what you would put on for a meal at home.

At my first cannery meal, I was amazed to see people run into the dining room, put an arm around all of the serving dishes, scoot them to their place, serve themselves quickly, wolf down their food, jump up and leave. I had never seen that approach to food before. I was sure my Aunt Millie would have fainted dead away at the sight. After a few days of my "would you please pass" being lost in the pandemonium I became more aggressive. Later at home Lydia said, "Wilma! For heavens sake, no one is going to take your food away from you." I guess I had become more aggressive than I realized.

The cannery hired a small crew to start the season. Just before the run hit they would send a boat into Anchorage and hire 10 or 15 people. I am not sure what the recruiting methods were and I don't think they were actually Shanghaied like you see in the movies, but sometimes when this incoming crew sobered up they were very surprised to find themselves on a boat headed for an island where there were no alcoholic refreshments available.

One of these men bore an uncanny resemblance to Frankenstein's monster. When I first saw him in the dining room he had a terrible hangover. His hands shook so badly it sounded like sleigh bells when he tried to set his coffee cup on the saucer. They put him to work wheeling the stacks of coolers in and out of the retorts. These huge pressure cookers (retorts) released steam in a giant hissing cloud when the cooking cycle was complete.

About the third day, the steam and noise sent this man's poor wine-soaked brain back to World War I where he had been shell-shocked. His reaction was to start fighting the war all over again. The first move was to try and burn out the enemy camp, which unfortunately was the men's bunkhouse. This got everyone's attention. Luckily the fire was put out without too much damage.

They got him under control and put handcuffs on him. It was difficult finding a place to keep him where he wouldn't hurt himself or anyone else until he could be transported. They settled on a spot in the can loft where the cases of unfinished cans were stored about forty feet directly in front of my working position on the reformer machine.

Somehow the man managed to climb on top of the boxes. They had tied a piece of line to the rafter and attached it to his hand cuffs to keep him from wandering. He tried to climb up this rope but wasn't strong enough. His next move was to chase the imaginary enemy around on the top of the stacked boxes, creeping, attacking and beating them. He was so realistic about this I got to where I could almost see the unfortunate individual he was attacking.

The boy from the kitchen who brought his meals had to be very careful not to be one of the enemy who got caught. In spite of feeling very sorry for the poor man, I was glad when they took him away for proper medical attention.

The "reformer" I ran was an interesting machine. It made the little can carcasses that were shipped flat round again. I loved my job because it was dry and warm in the can loft and there was only about a week in mid-July when we did 16 hours a day. Other times we had fun. It was a wonderful summer and I went home 16 years old with $387.00.

Everyone was excited to be going home after five weeks at the cannery. About five hours out of Snug Harbor, we began to see the hills of Homer. They lay basking in the summer sun, arrayed in their fuchsia cloak of fireweed. What a sight to see.

It was getting harder all of the time to hate Alaska but I was still working at it.

Chapter 12

Settling In

Eight of us started high school September of 1941 in the brand-new school that had been built that summer. The school policy was to teach two high school classes each year and this year they were teaching sophomore and senior classes. Although I didn't have my freshman credits I took the sophomore classes.

I hated biology with a passion and did not want to take it. It didn't take me too long to figure out that what I wanted had very little to do with what happened. The other subjects were fine, even geometry. I loved English and it's a good thing, because for any sort of misconduct you had to write a theme. Since doing my own thinking was already a habit of mine, my main subject became creative writing.

That summer, Stock Co. got the contract to build an airport in Homer so the mail planes wouldn't have to land on the beach any more. Of all of the major jobs ever done in Homer I would say that job put more actual dollars into the town than any other that I can remember since. The local men drove trucks and the welder was Jack English from Seldovia. There were some imported "cat-skinners" (Caterpillar drivers) and a big guy, Murve Broughten, who ran the dragline.

Two newcomers that came to town on that project were Vaino Salo, the head mechanic, and Hank Anderson, the camp cook. They both stayed after the airport was completed and lived out their years here. Mr. Stock, the head of the construction company, bought the old Homer grade school building and made it into his home. He set it next door to the camp buildings to be able to have electricity off of a common light plant since city electricity was still far in the future.

Fall was a busy time. The winter grocery order came in on the boat and had to be put away on the shelves upstairs.

The butter barrel went on the back porch where it was cool. The brine was salty enough it didn't freeze solid but as the weather became colder I hated sticking my hand into that icy brine to get out a pound of butter.

Daddy went hunting and we had moose meat to care for. Some we ground into hamburger, forming it into patties before putting it in the cans. Some we chopped in pieces and canned for stews or sandwiches. The steaks we cooked thoroughly and put them into a bucket. We then rendered out moose fat to pour over them to preserve them. The disadvantage being if you preferred your steak medium rare you were out of luck. Some large chunks of meat were put into an empty butter barrel and corned.

We went razor-clam digging on the Spit and canned them. There were blueberries, lowbush cranberries and moss berries to be gathered to make jams and jellies or to be canned for pies and cobblers.

Our cook stove burned coal. The coal shed had to be filled before winter storms put a coating of ice over the beaches. It took a lot of coal to get through the winter. Since I loved to drive the truck, getting coal was something us kids were often involved in.

We developed a system for loading coal. When we got to the beach I put "Lena" in compound gear and set my now 6-year- old brother Sonny in the driver's seat to steer while we walked alongside picking up pieces of coal and tossing them on the truck.

When it was full, I would relieve Sonny of the driving job and we would head home to unload it into the coal shed for the cold winter days ahead. Sometimes, if it was a nice day, we would build a fire and roast wieners when the truck was loaded before heading for home.

All of these different hunt-and-gather operations were supervised by Tuffy, always near and watchful or running alongside the truck. He was such a good friend. I can't think of him even today without getting a lump in my throat.

In October 1941, Guy Waddell wanted to sell his little Chevrolet coupe and I wanted it, but it would take all of the money I had left. Lydia suggested she buy a half interest and I teach her to drive. I suspect now, being the intelligent lady she was, she thought it might serve to keep a lid on my adventuresome spirit if she was half owner.

We did buy the car. Teaching Lydia to drive was another matter. She was my one total failure of the many people I taught to drive. In low gear she was fine, then I would tell her to push in the clutch and put it in second. "No," she would say in a terrified voice, as the starved car hopped along. No amount of reasoning, or begging, or coaxing, would budge her.

"Why won't you put it in second or give it any gas?" I would ask in what I hoped sounded like a patient voice. "Because it will go too fast," she answered, clutching the steering wheel in sheer terror. It was not until I stopped trying to teach her that things got back to normal at home and I was no longer the enemy. We both loved the car. I would drive her places and pick her up when she wanted. It worked out fine.

On the morning of December 7, 1941, Loma and I were sprawled on the living room rug pouring over a new Chicago Mail Order catalog that had just come in the mail off of the *Cordova*. Suddenly Lil was knocking on the door and pushing it open. I started to say "hi" but the look on her face stopped me cold. She hurried to the radio saying over her shoulder, "They have bombed Pearl Harbor!"

"Who bombed Pearl Harbor?"

"The Japs."

She tuned in a station that was saying things about the bombing in that "special emergency voice," the one that strikes terror to your heart. We sat listening, making comments, with our minds racing to think what changes it would make in our own lives.

"Do you think they'll bomb the *Cordova*?" Loma asked in a scared little voice.

"Maybe," I answered slowly, trying to adjust my mind to these new developments. "I don't know. I never did war before."

The first actual signs of war touched our lives when some of the boys got their draft notices. The first group to be called were the cat-skinners and operators from the airport job. We gave a farewell dance for them on President Roosevelt's birthday, the 13th of January, 1942.

In a few weeks another group was called. This time it was the hometown boys. The boat came to the front beach to pick them up and take them to Seward. It was a pretty, sunny day. Alice Bellamy brought her husband, Ben, and brother, Stanley Woodman, down off of the hill. Dorothy Gray brought her husband, Glenn, and brother, Lloyd Maxwell, down. Lil and I brought her brother, Bob Walli. Most everyone tried to keep it light, but the tears came anyway as the boys threw their duffels into the skiff and pushed off the beach. The skiff moved across the glistening blue water toward the boat that would take them to the Army. In time we got them all back in good shape, but that day we didn't know it would be that way.

Friends and family in the States wrote of things like rationing of gas, sugar, butter and meat. For us, tires were a little hard to get sometimes but we didn't have rationing. It would have been difficult to manage in Alaska because most places stocked their groceries annually.

Rationing rumors would have made a lot more sense if it weren't for the stories that drifted back to us. One man, a civilian employee at a military base whose job was to haul out loads of excess fuel and burn it, made the sad mistake of filling the fuel tank of a poor family. He served a year in prison for this "error" in judgment. Another local man stopped buying war bonds when he was ordered to dig a hole with the dragline that was then filled with new batteries and tires. So went the war.

About this time, a Territorial Policeman came to town and stood in front of the post office. As we went to pick up our mail he went over to each car and, of all things, that crazy man wanted us all to put current licenses on our cars. Someone hurried off to the phone and rang a general alarm to tell everyone to steer clear of that area but he persisted and stayed for days. Before that you could tell when each vehicle had come to Homer because that was the year on the license plate. In the end we all bowed to the law, besides a week without mail is quite a while.

Chapter 13

On My Own

I couldn't seem to keep my mind on school. I kept thinking I needed to get a job. In the spring of 1942 I decided to go to work for Pete and Opal James, at the little restaurant that is now the Waterfront. At that time it was only two small rooms and a small upstairs. I worked for them for several months, saved some money and decided it was time for me to go back to the "States."

I sold my share of the car to Lydia and flew to Anchorage en route to Seattle. During the war years it was necessary to go through paperwork for clearance. My father was not happy with me for leaving.

Looking back, I think I had been subjected to so many different people's rules in my life I wasn't willing to adjust another time. I would rather have scrubbed floors, than to learn someone else's do's and don'ts. I wasn't mad at anyone, I was just tired of it all and wanted to do my own thinking for a change.

In Anchorage, I was to stay with Lydia's sister, Tess, and her husband until I left on the train for Seward. They were very nice to me. I planned to be there about a week to do the paperwork and get my ticket.

The second evening I was in town, I got a call from Dick Neirstimer. Dick had been a cat-skinner on the Homer Airport job and was now stationed in Anchorage at Fort Richardson. Some of our mutual friends were getting together at the South Seas that evening. Would I like to go along?

The South Seas was a popular local night club and I was a little nervous about going night clubbing but if you are going to be grown up you might as well get on with it. The evening had barely begun when everyone started coaxing me to stay in Anchorage and go to work. They reminded me I might have trouble getting work "Stateside" because I was only 16.

When Dick took me home that evening he made me promise to try at least one place to find work and stay in Alaska. Well, it wouldn't hurt to try.

The following morning, I pinned my long hair up on top of my head, put on lipstick, earrings and high heels, and set forth to keep my promise. Help was hard to get in those war years and employers didn't spend much time worrying about details like age, but I wanted to look at least 18, to be on the safe side. In all likelihood, I probably looked 16, trying to look 18.

At 10 a.m. on that November morning in 1942, I walked into the Merchants Cafe on Fourth in Anchorage. Hans, the owner, was standing at the cash register, punching it with a vengeance. Around his neck hung an untied, white apron. The man looked a bit harried. There was not another soul in the place, which gave me the courage to say in an unsure little voice, "Could you use some help?"

He pulled off the apron handed it to me and said, "Yes! Now."

Probably one of the shortest job interviews in history. I was a little startled by things happening so fast. I asked to come back in an hour. He said okay and I retreated. Later I found out two of his waitresses had gotten in a fight behind the counter the evening before. One waitress ended up in the hospital, the other he fired, thus paving the way for my speedy employment.

I will never forget that day if I live to be 100 years old. I went back to the cafe at 11 a.m. Another waitress had come in and she immediately started telling me where things were with a sense of urgency that I didn't see any reason for at the time. The butter came in uncut full one-pound cubes which had to be cut into pats and stacked on plates. Coffee was made in huge pots. Each thing was new to me. I soon found out why all the preparation.

84

About 11:45 a.m. all hell broke loose. This was the main eating place for every construction man in Anchorage and there were a lot of them. There was a horseshoe-shaped counter with twenty stools and six big booths that would accommodate six people each. At times there was even someone on their knees at the end of the table.

It would have been hell for a seasoned waitress in low-heeled shoes. I was a green waitress in high-heeled shoes and it was a nightmare. Customers stood three deep behind each stool. One slid out, another slid in. I tried to tell by their expression whether they'd eaten. I wasn't familiar with the menu or prices. As if there weren't enough problems, the eight o'clock waitress didn't show up.

The cook seemed to have a problem with my method of ordering. I would approach the cook's counter and say quietly to that plump Italian cook who had twenty-five orders ahead, "Sir, sir, would you mind fixing an order of pork chops, please?" He stopped cold and stared at me.

"Just singa out when you coma through the door. You say 'pork chopsa ona one,'" he said slowly.

"Y-y-yes," I stammered. But some things are built in. The second day when I gave him my polite order he came from behind the chef's table, shouting and wielding a meat cleaver over his head.

"Cana you holler?" he screamed.

I was so terrified, I could hardly speak, but I must have made an affirmative squeak because he continued his tirade.

"When you coma through that door, you singa out like the other girls do. You gotta that?"

From that day on I never came into that kitchen that my tummy didn't tie in a knot. I tried hard to please him. I am sure he would be very surprised to find that I spent the next 25 years doing waitress work and cooking. In later years, when I was cooking, I tried to temper my reactions to green waitresses with memories of that day.

I had another problem. During my vegetarian years with my Adventist aunt and uncle I had never seen a pork chop. I didn't know what they looked like. I knew a hamburger and a steak but the rest was by guess and by golly.

I worked until midnight while the juke box played "Moonlight Cocktails," the popular song of the day, over, and over, and over. Even today I associate that song with blistered feet and confusion.

When I left work that night, I smiled sweetly, said goodnight, walked about half a block where I hoped I was out of sight of any of the restaurant patrons. I took a deep breath, pulled off those miserable high-heeled shoes and put them in my pockets. Even though it was quite chilly the cool cement felt wonderful to my blistered feet. When I tried to put my shoes back on to cross the graveled street, I thought I would cry.

I hurt so bad I even thought of giving up and going back to school in Homer, but I got over that by morning. I made it to Tessie's house, soaked my feet, and crawled into bed. That day gave the word "tired" a brand new meaning for me. I had worked at the Merchants Cafe for a week when Hans motioned for me to come over and talk to him. Instinctively I knew what was coming and said, "You don't have to tell me that I am in over my boot tops."

He smiled. "You have come a long way this week, but it is just too high speed until you have more experience."

I agreed and we parted friends. Later on, I worked several relief shifts for him with much better results.

The M&M Cafe was about three blocks away. It was smaller, and in minutes I had a job there. It was a little hole-in-the-wall place and Brownie, the owner, was also the cook.

I remember one incident when Brownie reprimanded me: A soldier had come in and ordered a hamburger. He was the octopus type, all hands and wanting to pat things that weren't on the menu. After a certain amount of dodging I suggested that he keep his hands on his hamburger.

"Don't give me that hard-to-get stuff. You waitresses are all alike," was his smart alec answer.

Never say things like that to a waitress armed with a catsup bottle. Brownie heard the soldier's comment, anticipated my reaction, and rushed out of the kitchen, coming up behind me just as I raised the catsup bottle over my shoulder to get a really good swing. I planned to fracture that young man's skull. Brownie grabbed the bottle and sent the young man away, suggesting that he do his business elsewhere in the future. Then he turned to me and said "Don't take everything so personally."

If I was going to work in Anchorage I needed to make some other arrangements and not impose on Bill and Tessie. With no difficulty I rented a small two-room house on East B now called Barrow, and settled in. When I finished putting up my curtains I sat down and looked around my very first house. It seemed like this was the moment I had been waiting for since that day in Oregon under the Japanese quince bush when I realized I was going to have to figure out a lot of things for myself. My soul was my own at last. I couldn't have been happier.

I missed Loma and, whenever my stubborn mind would allow it, I missed Homer too. I comforted myself thinking Homer was only 45 minutes away in Star Airline's Stinson A. I lived on my tips and saved my checks for rent, water and lights for the first time.

With the war going on and fifty thousand transient GIs stationed at Fort Richardson, Anchorage was a wide open town. It was the jumping off place to the Aleutians. I was 16 years old. It would have been a good place to go to hell in a hand basket, but I was lucky.

My people kept saying prayers for me and my guardian angel hung in there. I'm afraid I must have given her several headaches. I'm sure that my grandmother, my aunt and uncle, and my father never thought I had listened to any of their instructions. But some of it had stuck in my little brain though and saw me through the tough times. Teen-agers *can* hear, it is just that it usually has a delayed action.

I hadn't been in Anchorage long when a young soldier asked me to go dancing. I was off work that night. It sounded fun and I agreed. He was a nice guy and, under different circumstances, we would have had a great time. But whenever anyone asked me to dance, that long, tall Texan's reaction was to flatten the asking party. Now that certainly can break up an evening. I took a taxi home and made a decision that when I wanted to dance I would just drop in and dance with everybody then disappear. It worked.

The cab I called that night was a White Top. It was driven by the company owner, an older man who became my very good friend. His name was Reese Tatro and he asked me if I would like to dispatch cabs for him on busy nights. There were no radios yet so the dispatcher took down the info and waited

87

for a cabby to show or call in so it was important to have someone there. I agreed to do it a couple of hours after I got off work at my other job.

He had raised a family and he gave me a lot of good advice. The amazing thing is that I listened. I tried not to cringe at Reese's bluntness and lack of diplomacy, bless his heart. If I started showing a special interest in anyone, Reese would say, "Now you think about this a lot. When you get serious about someone, you are stuck with them an awful long time. It is important they wear well. This other stuff wears off with time."

Reese missed his wife terribly. She had died two years before. He said sadly, "I loved that lady when I married her, but five years down the road, I loved her more and, in twenty years more yet. When I lost her, half of me died."

He always took me home after I had worked for him instead of letting the young and eager. Just a protective measure but it was thoughtful of him and I appreciated it.

Many years later I met a middle-aged man in Anchorage who somehow looked familiar. I asked his name. When he said "Reese Tatro," I told him I had known his father during the war years and what a very special person he was.

I found working evenings saved a lot of problems. The soldiers were lonely and didn't understand "No" when they asked for a date. I was still working for Brownie at the M&M eight to five when I went to work evenings for Fred and Marie Schotte at their combination drugstore and soda fountain from 5:15 till 11 p.m. Good thing it was only three blocks away. I usually ran to get there on time.

One winter evening at Schotte's I got a lesson I would remember for a lifetime. When you are 16 and there are thousands of GIs coming in where you work it is easy to listen to their good-natured baloney. Early on my shift at the soda fountain I was busy filling up containers and getting ready for a busy evening. A young GI sat at the counter sipping his milk shake and giving me line number 33 — the one that goes, "You have the prettiest blue eyes I have ever seen. Your hair has such beautiful highlights. Your smile makes my heart turn over." I will admit he sounded sincere, and I was listening. Several people came in and I got busy.

In those days, there were some girls around Anchorage that the fellows had special names for. One was a little Native girl with protruding teeth that they called "Buck Tooth Annie." About the time I got busy, Annie came in and sat down by the line-number-33 guy. Some place through the bits of conversation that drifted over to me, I heard him repeating word for word what he had said to me a half hour before. That miserable wretch didn't even have the decency to change the wording. I had to laugh and say to myself "so much for your over-inflated ego, Wilma." The soldier paid for her Coke, and they strolled out the door arm in arm.

That lesson helped me remember that these boys were lonely and far away from home, and that I should not attach much significance to their chatter. It kept my feet firmly on the ground.

When I left Anchorage, the boys in the 75th Coast Artillery gave me a plaque. It was about two feet across. On one side was the Alaska Defense Command Insignia, and on the back they had written: "To little Sister who is always there to write a letter to our mom, pick out a present for our sister and etc." The rest was covered with signatures.

They were a great bunch of guys. I was so pleased with their gift. I thought they were very grown up until I looked at their pictures years later. It seemed so unfair when their young faces looked out of those pictures at me to think they were sent off to fight a war. When I think of the ones who didn't come back, I have a little problem with the handling of the post World War II foreign policy.

The shortest way home from work was down C Street, past the houses of ill repute, past the Ambassador Club and through a vacant, wooded lot. The fact that C Street was not a good neighborhood didn't seem to worry me. Jogging hadn't come into style as yet, so I just ran from my job home. If anyone tried to grab me, someone would always say, "Leave that kid alone." See, God does watch over little fools.

After the "do-gooders" of the town got the houses closed down, the situation became very dangerous. A little girl was raped and murdered in the vacant lot that I had run home through moments before. Reese read about it in the paper and after that he'd saunter into the soda fountain around closing time, order a Coke, say he "just happened to be in the neighborhood" and would I like a ride home. I just know my guardian angel prompted that dear man.

Since I have become a parent, I know how my poor father and Lydia must have worried about me living in Anchorage at such a young age.

By June 1942 I had been working 15 hours a day for months, and I was exhausted. One day I quit all of my jobs, and went home to Homer on Hiney Berger's boat the *Kasilof*. It was my first trip through the Forelands and I was facinated with the fact the tide ran so hard the skipper had to keep the engine going full bore just to hold our position until the tide turned. We made a stop at Kenai to let off passengers and freight then moved on to Kasilof, Hiney's home dock. The next stop was Homer and I found myself straining my eyes for a first glimpse. I was glad to be back. At first my dad was a little reserved but he was getting used to me surviving on my own.

I wasn't home long before I realized you can never go back in time because time and experience have made you a different person. I missed my little house and my total independence.

Two weeks later, I was on the way to Snug Harbor again. This time Lil went along and that made it more fun. Snug Harbor was a neat, well-kept place, powered primarily by water. Erick Freibrock, the owner, deserves a great deal of credit for his general layout of the cannery. Economically and systematically, he ran a tight ship.

There were three boats tendering for Snug Harbor. The *Orient*, with Ing still skippering, the *Venus* and the *Lillian J*. The skipper on the *Venus* had a running battle with the tide that ran hard by the dock. In the end, the deck hands would moan, grab the pike pole and make the landing.

The *Lillian J* was the baby of the fleet, about a 50-footer. Hoogy Foster, whose father owned an interest in the cannery, skippered it.

Each day we would watch for the tenders, anxious to know how many fish they had aboard so we would know about how long we would be working the next day. Even from a distance, it was easy to tell which boat it was.

The *Orient* had a "top house" and would be rolling from side to side. The *Venus* bobbed over one wave after another. The *Lillian J* came through each wave with the mast hardly moving up or down.

All of the cannery workers were conscious of the war, so I thought it would be a good idea to go over things with Lil in case the Japanese started dropping out of the sky. We discussed it a little, then I said, "Now if there is an invasion, what is the first thing you put into our getaway pack?"

I thought she would immediately say food, but Lil, who was very blond, had a different answer.

"My eyebrow pencil," was her immediate response. So much for that drill. At least if she was captured she would be a beautiful prisoner.

When we went home that year, it was on the *Venus* in the teeth of a howling gale. Everyone was sick five minutes after we left Tuxedni Bay, partly from the weather and partly from the smell of diesel in the bilges. It made for a very unpleasant journey and we were glad when it was over.

Since quitting high school I had kept studying on my own. That fall I took a typing course in the hope that it might help me find a better job. My dad let me use his typewriter and it seemed to come easy to me. Now shorthand was a whole different matter. It just would not sink into my head no matter how hard I tried.

That fall, after carefully counting my cannery earned dollars, I bought a Lot on the CT road for $215. The CT road that originally followed Henry Ohlsen's hay trail is now called Bartlett Street. I think it was the first real subdivision in Homer, although Pa Svedlund had sold off pieces of his land earlier. For once I had done something right as far as Daddy was concerned. Then I went back to Anchorage to work.

In Anchorage I looked for a job where I could put my newly acquired typing skill to work. I found that job working for the Civil Aeronautics Authority, called the CAA, the forerunner of the FAA. At that time, their offices were in the Federal Building in downtown Anchorage. I worked as a switchboard operator and file clerk.

I liked the job and met a lot of Alaskans who became well known: Francis Mayer, later of Manley & Mayer Architectural Services, who designed so many of the larger buildings in Anchorage. Earl Norris, who liked, even then, to show pictures of his dog team and of a girl he had met named Natalie. He would go on to marry Natalie and become well known as a dog musher. Jack Jefford and Harold Gillam, who were famous bush pilots.

I once rode to Homer with Jack on a CAA plane. (Jack's book "Winging It" is just great.) Johnny Hooper, an engineer for the CAA, I had met in Homer when he was instrumental in laying out the Homer Airport.

Flying had been a part of my life since coming to Alaska. Because of the broad expanses of country in Alaska that have no road access we are a very aviation-minded country. In my spare time that winter of 1942, I went out to Merrill Field and took flying lessons from Dick Miller at Jack Carr's Flying Service.

It was a gray winter day with a good 15-knot cross wind when I went out to Merrill for my initial flight. I had purchased several books on aviation procedures and absorbed them fully before I went to take my first lesson. I thought if I sounded like I had an idea what I was doing maybe I wouldn't be asked about my age. Is that called baffling 'em with BS? It is probably a good thing they didn't ask me to exhibit that vast knowlege I had stored up.

The first thing the instructor had me do was shoot, or practice, landings. There was only one runway at that time, so we didn't have any options in dealing with the cross wind. If I thought he would cut me any slack because it was my first lesson and the weather was lousy, I soon knew better. I paid my $16 for the hour and he certainly gave me my money's worth. He showed me how to "side slip" into the wind and then sat leisurely back while I tried it. I was nervous! At one point I said, "Oh God."

Dick glanced over at me and said in a firm voice, "Look, God don't land this airplane, and neither do I. You do!"

I mumbled something about him never getting a chance to die in bed, that some fool student would get him killed but he bluffed me out. I landed, and again, and again.

"Aren't these conditions a little extreme?" I asked at one point.

"It will toughen you up faster," he said, grinning. Good theory I guess, though I was not all for it at the time.

One lovely sunny day, we strapped on parachutes and went up for loops, spins and stalls. I loved it, and all went well, until we had finished the lesson and I asked, "Dick, can I bail out?" He probably helped me get older than 17 when he said, "Good grief, no. There are probably moths in these old parachutes." Nothing like being prepared.

When I had my eight hours dual time in we took off on a routine flight to practice landings, I thought.

"Take it over to the Cambell Creek strip," Dick said as we took off from Merrill.

"Okay."

I was happy about shooting landings at Cambell Creek strip because I didn't have to worry about the control tower and there were very few other aircraft on that strip. I flew over, happily chattering about the movie I had seen the night before called *Flight to Freedom*, about Amelia Earhardt. When I landed Dick said, "Stop a minute." I did and he got out.

"Go for it, kid," he said, and smiled. I almost panicked.

"Oh, Dick, don't leave me," I pleaded.

He laughed. "You'll do fine. Besides you can't solo with your instructor along."

I talked to myself during the whole ordeal. "Steady, Wilma, full throttle, okay now, the tail is up, pull back the stick, easy, easy," and so on until I was up, around, and back on the ground. Dick gave me my short snorter that day. That is a dollar bill that every body signs for a newly soloed pilot. I was a pretty proud kid. Larry Flayheart and Curly McDonald, pilots for Woodley Airways at the time, were at the hangar when I came in and they signed it. I couldn't stop smiling.

I have always hated to fly over water and Dick knew it. After I was flying alone logging some hours I would say, "I think I'll fly to Homer today."

Dick would laugh and say, "If you ever try I'll know right where to find you. That would be at 20,000 feet just this side of Turnagain Arm." Probably right too.

I never got my license. Partly because of the money part and partly because of having to go into that completely enclosed link trainer to get my instrument hours. It sets my claustrophobia into overdrive. Down through the years I have flown occasionally.

I got up one morning and decided I had waited long enough to do what I said I would do when I came to Alaska: Go south. I quit my job, bought a ticket on the *Columbia* to Seattle and headed for Oregon to see Gram. I had grown up enough I wanted to tell her personally I realized how much she had done for me.

Those were such good years. I loved making my own decisions and not being told constantly to appreciate everything anyone did for me. It wasn't that I didn't appreciate things. I did. I just hated being told that over and over. Every person should have a time in their life when neither Dad nor Mom, aunts nor uncles, husbands nor children are governing.

It was wartime and you had to have a passport with your picture on it and be okayed before you could travel. I went through the red tape quickly and was ready to go. I didn't have much money, but, ever the optimist, I launched out.

Getting aboard the passenger boat *Columbia* was a rather cloak-and-dagger type of operation. I was told when to come to Seward but not when the boat would leave. That was a military secret. There was a military checkpoint to pass through before going aboard. At this point, the officials read your papers, scrutinized you, checked you and your bags very carefully. They didn't allow any radios, alcoholic beverages or papers saying you were a spy.

The windows of the ship were painted black to avoid any light shining out at night. There were little canvas rooms at the dining room entrances that you stepped into before opening the door to keep the light from shining out.

After due process, they dropped the lines, and we pulled away from the dock. Well I had done it. I wasn't going to stay in Alaska. I was headed south. Where was that feeling of elation? I suddenly realized that there was a tear trickling down my cheek.

What is this, Wilma? You said you weren't going to stay in this country. You are on your way south. Now why aren't you happy? Then it finaly dawned on me. I *was away from home*!

What is it that makes Alaska so special? I thought about that question. There are so many things. The people whose word is their bond. The sun sinking in the western sky, painting a radiant path of yellows and oranges across Cook Inlet's mottled waters. The clean stillness of a winter night when the moon makes little sparkles on the snow and your snowshoes make crunchy noises as you trot along. The smell of good moose meat stew simmering on the back of the oil range.

I stood on the deck of the *Columbia* watching Seward fade in the distance, tears running down my face. I knew and admitted, at last, that I was hooked on Alaska. How was it that Robert Service said it? "You hate it like hell for a season and then you are worse than the worst." I started planning my return before we cleared Resurrection Bay.

For the time being, however, there was nothing to do but enjoy the trip. In Ketchikan, after a trip ashore we were checked carefully as we reboarded the ship to see we had no alcoholic beverages. I came through the shakedown, boarded and stood at the rail with the others watching the procedure. The searcher was giving a young man who was obviously intoxicated a thorough going over when he found a bottle taped to the man's leg.

"You can't take a bottle aboard." The official said.

"But it ish *my* bottle. I paid for it and it'sh good shtuff," pleaded the young man, weaving slightly.

"It's only yours until you start up that gangplank. Then it's mine and I am going to throw it overboard," the searcher said, in a very firm voice.

"Oh, but you can't do that, it would be shuch a waste." But the young man was now removing the bottle from his leg. He looked at the bottle sadly, then taking off the top he said, "I guessh I better drink it."

With grim determination he chug-a-lugged that bottle, threw the empty overboard and started up the gangplank.

Even with his stubborn determination he ended upon his hands and knees. We all stood at the rail shouting encouragement.

"Come on, you can make it, just a little ways further." Nothing like having a rooting section when you have a tough job to do. It was two days before I saw him in the dining room again and he still didn't look at all well.

After a week on the boat, we arrived in Seattle. Today we board a plane, have a nice lunch, read a little and we are there. The boat trips were definitely more time consuming. I enjoyed the trip south, but I knew that I would enjoy the trip *home* more.

Chapter 14

Return to South 48

My "stateside" journey touched Dallas, where I visited Gram and friends I had gone to school with. They listened in awe as I told them stories about Alaska. Every time I talked about Homer in that far away northland I got more homesick.

When I got to Walla Walla I stayed with my aunt and uncle, visited Merlie and her husband and kids, and decided to go to beauty school while I was there. I rented a little apartment for $15 per month in one of the big old houses near the church in Walla Walla where I had gone to school. Still optimistic that I would be able to find some work to help my dwindling finances, I started beauty school. My Aunt Millie and Uncle Bill were always bringing me canned fruit and vegetables from their home-canned supplies, which helped stretch dollars. I finally had to face the fact there were no jobs. Anything available was quickly taken by military wives. I lasted four months studying hard and being frugal, but with no daylight showing at the end of the tunnel it was time for action. I had $25 left to buy a bus ticket to Seattle and survive on till I could get work.

I knew a lady in Seattle and I went directly there. I was able to rent a room with cooking privileges. I guess I have an honest face, because she agreed to trust me for the money for the room until I got work.

After a good night's sleep I caught the number 15 bus to downtown Seattle to see if I could solve the job situation. As I rounded the corner near the employment agency I was shocked to see the long line of people. With a sinking heart I joined them. I breathed a sigh of relief when I was hired as a rivet bucker on B-17s at Boeing. You can tell that the requirements weren't too tough as my only experience with rivets was when Merlie and I had made the harness for the goat, although I didn't put that on the form that I filled out. Today they would probably require a degree in engineering and four years of college to do the same thing.

Thanks to the fact that I could get to work for a quarter and a bus transfer on Seattle's transit system I was able to make it to my first payday. My grocery shopping to see me through consisted of two loaves of bread, a quart of sandwich spread and a bag of apples.

When I got my first check I stopped at the Triple X, ate two big hamburgers and drank a cherry milk shake. What a wonderful celebration! After I paid my rent for two weeks I was back on my previous diet.

Boeing was different than anything I had done before. I found myself in the B-17 tail and fuselage area armed with a small rectangular metal bar about 2 1/2 inches by 5 inches. One end of the bar was square, the other end slanted in order to get into smaller areas. The pieces of aluminum skin that were to cover the metal skeleton of the plane just dropped out of the sky via overhead crane. The skin had rivet-size holes around the outside edge and lines of holes where it would attach to the ribs.

Frenchie, the riveter I was assigned to work with, gave directions to the crane as it swung the skin into place and we were ready for business. When I try to remember what he looked like, all I remember was he was nearly bald, wore glasses and scowled a lot. There is a possibility that the scowl came from having to deal with the young and inexperienced. However he was a good riveter and could climb around that tail and fuselage section like a monkey.

Hearing the instructions was impossible but I got the idea from his wild motions that he wanted me to climb inside the metal skeleton onto the boards placed on the ribs. I had just gotten in there when he put a rivet in one of the corner holes and hit it with the rivet gun.

Even in the din, that sound came through like New Year's Eve in a boiler factory.

As I hurried to get the bar on the inside end of the rivet I got the distinct feeling that Frenchie wasn't really excited about breaking in a green kid. But I tried hard and soon our communication improved. The trick was to get the bar on the right rivet before he hit it. A little mistake in timing inspired me to do better before the racket totally destroyed my hearing.

A country kid used to peace and quiet, I worried a little about my sanity too. There were about a dozen jigs in the tail and fuselage area. Each one had at least two riveters and buckers. Overhead cranes whirred above, lifting out the completed projects and bringing in the skeletal beginnings of the next. That factory was the noisiest place I have ever been. I kept waiting for someone to break and go screaming out of the building and I hoped it wouldn't be me. No one would have heard them or noticed anyway.

Getting to work was an experience in itself. The buses were unbelievably crowded. The driver continually said "Step back in the bus, please" until things reached sardine conditions.

I got off swing shift at midnight one night and boarded the bus to go home. My ears were ringing from the noise, I was tired, people were stepping on my feet and jostling me about until I couldn't tolerate it another minute. I just lost it, rang the bell and got off of the bus.

In my extreme agitation I hadn't thought ahead. The buses quit running during the middle of the night. I was a good five or six miles from home. When the cool evening air and the quiet revived me I realized my predicament.

I had walked about 10 blocks, with the Washington tax tokens tied to my moccasin laces jingling, when I heard a long low whistle. My heart froze but my legs kept moving. I tried to look around me without turning my head. I saw to my right an area that was fenced. Behind the fence were a group of soldiers watching me. I didn't want to seem nervous, which I certainly was, so I didn't look back for another bus but my ears strained for the sound. The fence was a comfort but that was the longest block I walked that night. The bus picked up at two block intervals. Two more buses wheeled past as I ran between bus stops. My six mile (I'm guessing) stroll took me from Boeing plant number two in south Seattle to the Ballard Bridge area. It was very quiet and uncrowded and soothing to my ruffled nerves. However, there is nothing like a six-mile stroll in the middle of the night to improve one's tolerance of crowded buses.

I had Sunday off and my special, non-money-consuming entertainment was to walk down to the Fisherman's Terminal a few blocks away and talk to the guys I knew who were getting the tenders ready to go to Alaska. Was I homesick? You darn betcha.

I ate little, saved money and in May when I had the $104 for the Alaska Steamship Line and $30 extra I boarded the *Alaska* and headed home to God's country. I changed to the *Cordova* in Seward. When we docked at Red Mountain to unload mine supplies across the bay from Homer I jumped in a skiff with a fellow from Homer and headed home. The town looked so good, but it was the wonderful quiet I enjoyed most.

Chapter 15

Heartaches

In June when the tender came to pick us up, Loma and Lil both went with me to Snug Harbor and it was the best summer ever. We played volleyball, rowed around Chisik Island, worried about a Japanese invasion and, of course, flirted with the deck hands.

Fall came. Shirley Sholin was taking lab training at Providence Hospital in Anchorage and told me of an opening in the nurses' dining room. I went to work there, living in the hospital quarters in the old hospital building on L Street. The work was demanding and the nurses got a kick out of telling stories that kept me blushing, but they were great people.

One evening, Shirley had a date that she couldn't keep. She asked me if I would mind going up to the waiting room to tell her friend, Ted, she couldn't make it. When I got there, a young man was waiting. He stood about six feet tall, had dark hair, a little mustache, and the most beautiful brown eyes. If this was Ted I couldn't imagine why anyone would break a date with him.

"Are you Ted?" I asked.

"Well, no, but I am here on his behalf. You aren't Shirley, are you?"

"No, I'm not." And I gave Shirley's apologies.

"Ted can't make it either. He asked me to stop by and let Shirley know."

We struggled for something to say as though we were both reluctant to end the meeting. In the end, we sat in the waiting room talking while the Catholic sisters made nervous periodic pilgrimages by the door, checking to see that nothing was amiss. About two hours later he left to pick up the general he drove for. His name was Max and when he asked if I would like to have dinner with him the following evening, I, who had sworn not to date anymore in a town full of GIs, accepted and went back to my quarters smiling and humming a little tune.

It was wonderful. He brought out a different side of my personality. I was completely happy with his every decision.

If he would have said, "Let's go climb Mt. McKinley" I would have said, "Okay. What time?" People who have known me for a lifetime wouldn't even suspect I have that side. The next six months we dated nearly every night, my every waking hour revolved around him. I was totally in love with the guy. The whole world took on a rosy glow.

I changed jobs for a little better money and went back to work for the CAA. I rented a house over on 7th Street. It was much more of a house than the one I had rented before. I now had a kitchen, bedroom and a living room. Such luxury. Max would often deliver the general and then come by the house. I would have dinner ready, with background music such as the popular Lena Horne singing "Smoke Gets In Your Eyes" or another of her lovely soothing songs. It was idyllic.

But always there are the storm clouds ready to sprinkle a little rain into your life.

We were at a CAA dance one evening just before Christmas. I had a new blue dress and couldn't have been happier. Max was holding me in his arms as we danced to the "Blue Skirt Waltz" when a friend danced close and said to Max,"I hear you are shipping out. If I don't get to see you again, good luck, buddy."

I really yet don't remember much about the rest of the evening. I had to get out of the building with some kind of dignity. I probably even said "excuse me" as I made my way through the crowd. I was out the door and running. Max grabbed my coat and followed. When he caught up, he tried to reason with me. He told me he was afraid if he didn't take reassignment they would send him back to the Aleutians. After having been dumped on a beach at Cold Bay shortly after war was declared he had no desire to go back. That was the reason he had chosen reassignment to Camp Lucky Strike in England.

I wouldn't listen. I was destroyed. Why hadn't he told me? He must not love me if he wanted to transfer. I would hate to say we fought all night, but everything we discussed, we didn't agree on. He left at dawn, walking out of my life tall and straight in his khaki uniform, through the gray of the early morning. He, feeling that he was doing what he had to. Me, feeling he couldn't have made that decisions if he cared. I felt I had been a complete fool.

I couldn't eat. I couldn't sleep. I was having a hard time concentrating on anything. I put one foot ahead of the other until another day went by. I finally quit my job and went back to Homer. I walked on the beach a lot. Most of the old bunch were gone. But Lloyd Maxwell was still around. He had been given a medical discharge from the Army because of his vision. Lil had married Pat Miller, a CAA radio operator from Homer, and was now living in Roanoke, Virginia. Shirley had gone to Tacoma, Washington, to finish nurse's training. Loma was out in Oregon.

I dated Lloyd. He asked me to marry him. Max didn't write. I finally decided to get on with my life and married Lloyd. I really thought the marriage would work as we had always been good friends and he was a quiet Texas boy with many good qualities, that is as long as he was not drinking.

One day in 1944, just after the war was over, a letter came from Max and it said all of the things I had always wanted to hear him say. Some things just aren't meant to be.

Lloyd and I built a house on a piece of ground given to me by a friend of my dad's. We didn't know much about what we were doing but managed to get it built. It was a three bedroom, story-and-a-half Cape Cod, with two dormer windows built out of shiplap and celotex. I guess the worst thing was we didn't know about insulation. Those wonderful rolls of fiberglass insulation that keep us toasty warm today were still a thing of the future at that time. The end product of our building project was roomy, with large windows, lots of sun, and freeze-your-buns-off in the winter time. We didn't have the money to put in a well, so we hauled wash water from my dad's place and got our drinking water from the little spring behind the house.

Lloyd went to work for the Alaska Road Commission. At that time ARC consisted of an old gas-fired "cat" affectionately called the "Secret Weapon," a black Ford 2 1/2-yard dump truck called "Black Beauty" and one small pull grader. These things were parked on the corner of Lake Street and Pioneer long before the streets had a name. There was a tent house that held the extra parts. Maintenance on the machinery was done alongside the tent in whatever weather. No heated shop for these mechanical sons of Alaska.

Lloyd and I had only been married about six months when a girl I knew stopped by. She was a sixteen-year-old unwed mother with a 3-month-old baby girl. I felt very sorry for her. She was so young to be tied down.

"Why don't you leave the baby for a week and relax," I said. "I will take good care of her."

She jumped at the offer and went off to be a teen-ager for a week. When she came back I started to get the baby's things together but she said, "How would you like to keep her?"

I was really surprised, but said I would talk to Lloyd. That was how Carolee became a part of my life. She was a beautiful baby. I sewed clothes for her, read to her and enjoyed her very much.

It was a couple of months later that I got the first real insight into the monster that lay buried beneath Lloyd's quiet exterior. He had gone to bed and I was curled up in a chair in the living room reading a book. Suddenly he grabbed me by the hair and smashed his fist into my face. It was pretty bad. He had been raised in an abusive situation and the pattern continued.

Miserable as I was, time went by. I was delighted when his brother Harreld and his wife and two children came to stay with us while they built their house. Harreld was a very different sort of person than Lloyd and the time he and his wife Alice were with us was special. They both had a wonderful sense of humor and I desperately needed someone to laugh with. I loved them from the first. Things quieted down. Lloyd didn't show the other side of his personality when they were with us. I dreaded the day when their house was completed.

This arrangement had worked out so well that when Ambrey Blayden from Anchor Point asked if her daughter could stay at the house to attend high school I was pleased. Reenie was a welcome addition to our household and Lloyd was once again on his good behavior. She was fun, loved to cook and life was great with her around.

Reenie went home on Fridays to see her family at Anchor Point. I would take her as far as I could drive, usually to the top of Diamond Ridge. From there she would hike home for the weekend. One Friday afternoon I took her to Diamond Ridge but I was a little worried when snow flakes began to fall.

"Reenie, do you think you should go?" I asked with concern.

"Oh, don't worry about me. I will be home in no time. I know Daddy and Judge will be waiting with the sled at the Anchor River bridge," she answered reassuringly. She gave me a quick hug, shouldered into her pack sack and trotted off down the clearing where the road would be one day. The Judge she referred to was a huge collie that led her dad's team. He loved Reenie, and missed her when she was gone.

"Travel safe, kiddo. I'll be here at 3:00 p.m. on Sunday," I called after her.

I felt apprehensive about her going, although it was only snowing lightly. It would be a ten-mile run but she was in good physical condition and made the trip weekly. I waited there for about fifteen minutes in case she changed her mind. Then I turned the truck around and headed back to town. It was snowing harder even in that short time and the wind was picking up. I worried. The rest of the story I would hear on Sunday afternoon when I picked Reenie up.

The snowfall increased. Reenie ran faster until the swirling snow destroyed her visibility. The snow got deeper. She tried to stay on the path by the feel of the hard packed path beneath the snow. Her muscles were aching and she was getting very tired. Fighting the now driving force of the blizzard, she pushed on. Hoping she was still on the trail she punched holes in the knee-deep drifting snow. Her gloves were wet now and the miles of exertion were taking their toll. A snow loaded branch slapped her in the face. She would have to rest soon. So cold.

On the Anchor River end, Fred, Reenie's father, stood waiting for his daughter who was the apple of his eye. Occasionally he brushed the snow from the fur robes he had put on the sled to make her comfortable for the ride home. He knew the effort she put forth in order to spend the week-end at home and it pleased him. Judge whined, looking toward the woods.

Fred patted the dog, holding his collar, as he himself looked anxiously toward the wall of spruce trees. The velocity of the wind grew.

In the woods the snow hit Reenie in sheets. She was becoming confused. Just rest a few minutes. Maybe get out of the wind in under a tree. Yes, get in under the trees where it will be warm. Good idea. Slowly she sank down into the soft icy feathers of snow on the lee side of a tree.

Fred looked at his watch. Judge was barking now.

"What is it Judge? Do you think you ought to go find Reenie?"

The dog barked anxiously, looking first at his master and then toward the woods. Fred unsnapped the dog from the sled and he was gone like a shot.

Feeling warmer now. Good idea to rest. Should start on soon. What is that? Barking! Barking. A wet warm tongue. Am I being eaten? "Oh, Judge!"

Fred plowed his way through the drifts toward the barking sound. Trying to follow the trail of leaps the dog had made in the snow. Judge gave Reenie no peace, licking at her face, clawing at her clothes. She got up and with a firm grasp on his collar started staggering along toward her father's loving arms.

As this drama played itself out I was looking anxiously out of the window at the storm. Long before it gained blizzard proportions, I started pacing the floor. No telephone connections yet. No CB radios yet. I would stand no chance of trying to find her. I was so glad and relieved on Sunday afternoon to see her trotting down the trail, waving when she saw me.

In the spring when school let out Reenie and I went to Seldovia to work in the cannery. I hadn't been feeling well but attributed it to worry that the abuse would start again when Reenie went home. Lloyd wasn't happy about my decision to go to but didn't stop me.

Reenie, Carolee and I stayed briefly in Seldovia but got a chance to go with Bob Kester and his wife on his barge the *Eva May*. I was happy when I heard we would be processing on the upper end of Chisik Island about eight miles from the Snug Harbor cannery.

It was every bit as beautiful as I had remembered it to be. We had only been there a few days when we had a short work day and Reenie and I decided to walk down to my old stomping grounds, Snug Harbor Packing. It was a beautiful day. We took turns carrying Carolee when she got tired on that eight-mile stroll.

Arriving at the cannery, the first person we ran into was Phil Sutherland. He had been a deck hand on the *Orient*, when I was there earlier but was now skipper of the *Venus*. I introduced him to Reenie and it was electric. They couldn't keep their eyes off each other. That evening Phil walked us home to the other end of the island. The following day he came up in a skiff and was a frequent visitor the rest of the summer. One month later I stood up with them in Seldovia when they were married. When the tender went south in the fall Reenie went with Phil.

I had planned to leave Lloyd, if I could put enough money together, but I found out why I was not feeling well. I was pregnant. I went back home. I was going to make it work whether it would work or not. Tomorrow would be better.

My mother, during her year in the Salvation Army.

Me, just before heading north.

Four generations of Webb women. From front to back, me, Great-grandma Dunson, Gram and my mother, by the old oak tree at Dallas.

My mother and I, ready to go to Alaska

The Princess Pat

110

Freighter at Seldovia dock, 1926

The July babies celebrate their birthdays in Seldovia. In the back, left to right, Mrs. Morris holding Lynedd, Jetty Jean McLain and her mother, Enid McLain. In front, Raider Ursin, Peggy Peterson and me.

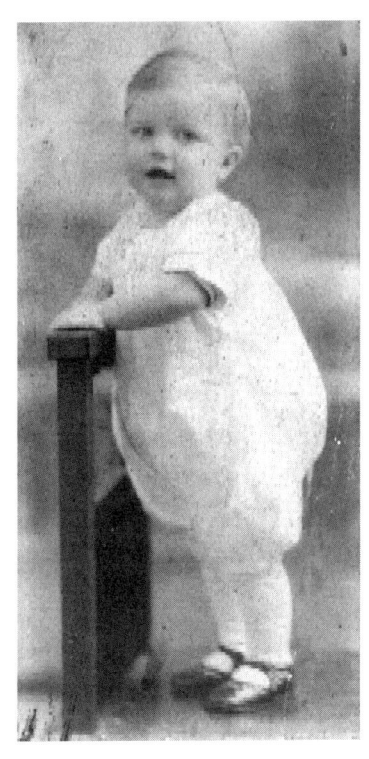

My little brother, Leland.

Me in Seldovia with the neighbor's dog.

Loma and I upon our arrival in Oregon at our grandparents' farm.

Loma and I, Merry Christmas at Dallas, Oregon.

Gram and Loma and I

113

Loma and I in Walla Walla

Taken in 1929, this was the only picture I had of Daddy until I saw him in 1941. Daddy is on the left.

114

Tuffy, with Sonny on the sled.

Lydia and Sonny.

Daddy and Lydia's house, 1941.

Auntie Walli

The new school at Homer, 1941.

116

Sonny and I just after I returned to Homer

Family portrait taken not long after Loma and I arrived in Homer. Left to right, me, Lydia, Daddy, Sonny and Loma.

Lil, fishing on the Stariski River.

Me in front of Gen. Down's car, the car that Max drove.

The Jeep that Inez and Larry Clendenen used to haul mail to Anchor Point.

Sterling Highway under construction.

Working on the road out of Homer. Old pull grader in operation.

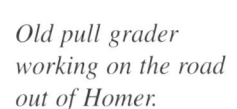

Old pull grader working on the road out of Homer.

The camp at Mile 8. Left to right, unidentified man, Chuck Carlson and Leonard Catlege.

119

Camp cook Rowena Tobias at the camp at Mile 8.

Left to right, back row — Halby, me holding Carmen, Merlie and her son Darrel; front row — Coni, Merlie's daughter Donna, and Tommy.

Lil, being beautiful, as always.

Chapter 16

Wanigan Days

In 1946 the Alaska Road Commission started in earnest to build the road out of Homer that would eventually connect with the Anchorage-Seward highway. People had been writing letters to Juneau for years expressing the need for such a road. The Alcan had been built during the war connecting Anchorage to the "States." Now with this last link, we would be able to drive from the towns and villages on the lower Kenai Peninsula to the "South 48."

The surveying of the basic roadway went both ways from Soldotna under Ralph Solberg's supervision. Jack VanZanten and his survey crew were sent in to straighten out problem areas. Working their way up the hill out of Homer, it was imperative they find a certain survey marker, in order to continue their work. The whole crew crawled around through the grass all of one day and into the next. Around noon on the second day, VanZanten came crawling through the tall grass to find Chuck Smith basking quietly in the warm summer sun.

"Chuck, get busy and find that stake," VanZanten scolded.

"I don't have to," Chuck answered.

VanZanten stopped short, thinking that he might have a rebellion on his hands.

"Chuck, why do you say that?" he asked seriously.

"Well, because I am sitting on it," Chuck said, scooting over to reveal the elusive survey marker.

It was a problem trying to find a route out of Homer that didn't exceed a seven percent grade. It had stymied the first crew.

When Jack came with his assistant, Chuck Smith, they soon agreed it couldn't be done. Time for Holley Sterling to come from the head office and take a look. Chuck ran rod for him, until he too agreed there were some places on that side hill that would simply have to be eight and a half percent and okayed it.

In Homer, we watched with interest as the town was occupied with new faces. Things were changing. We laughed at the stories the crew told on each other on Saturday nights when they hit town. One of the stories I remember was about Johnny Byrd when he was working with the crew surveying in the Anchor River area.

Someone shouted "Bear!" Without any encouragement everyone immediately found a tree. When the bear lost interest and wandered off, one by one the crew crawled from their safety perches....all except Johnny Byrd.

"John, where are you?" VanZanten called.

"I am up here in the tree," Johnny answered.

"Come on down. Why are you still up there?"

"I can't."

"Why not?"

"Well, I've got this armful of survey stakes," was John's answer.

They hadn't been a problem going up with the inspiration of a bear close behind but now with the emergency gone it was a different matter. The crew loved to tease him about that.

The Homer ARC crew slogged their way through from the end of the existing road toward Bidarka Creek. What a mess. That area was soggy wet and each foot gained was hard earned. Lloyd would try to ditch and crown, and another "cat" had to stand by to pull him out. A gravel truck would dump its load and have to be pulled back to safe footing as the gravel disappeared into the mire. They put planks down to back the trucks on and they, too, sank. I began to wonder if our wonderful road to the beyond would ever even get up the hill, but it did.

The Bidarka Creek fill and culvert were put in place in the fall of '46. That hurdle crossed, they pushed on up the side hill, putting in tote roads to get around the canyons. When it started freezing and the daylight hours were getting shorter, the crew drove to the top of the hill, then walked into the Diamond Creek area where they were working. By the time the equipment was started, they would be lucky to get four hours of actual working time.

Lloyd would come home caked with mud and I hauled water and washed and washed and washed. I packed lunches with hot coffee, an extra thermos to hold hot soup, sandwiches and cookies. That was my personal effort toward the progress of the Sterling Highway.

If they were careless about cleaning the mud from the bulldozer tracks the tracks froze solid. The next morning the "cat" couldn't budge until it was thawed out, which sometimes took hours, even when they went to the extreme measures of throwing diesel on the frozen mud and setting it on fire. The next step was to pray the fire thawed the tracks before the side curtains or oil residue from the engine caught fire. By late November, they were making so little headway they quit for the winter.

The ARC let out a contract for clearing five miles to some local men. One of the men was my dad, Tom Shelford, so we got first-hand reports on the progress each weekend. It was a miserably cold winter, with temperatures plunging to 25 degrees below zero. It was so cold the whole upper part of Kachemak Bay was frozen hard enough that at least one man walked across to the other side.

In the spring of 1947 the Alaska Road Commission moved equipment into Homer in force. Claude Rogers came in to boss the operation, bringing a crew of heavy-equipment operators with him. The first bunkhouse and cook shack were set up at the Homer office of ARC that had now moved across the road into Army surplus buildings. My uncle, Harry Barnum Sr., was the cook. There were DW-10s and Eukes to move gravel faster. D-8s with Hyster winches came off of the barge along with a couple of D-8s rigged to pull "cans." Lloyd graduated from the D-6 he had been running to a D-7 and he was pleased. It was an exciting time.

The first major project was number-one fill. It was awe inspiring to watch those big rigs move thousands of yards of dirt. I couldn't resist putting Carolee on the packboard and climbing up on the side hill to watch the progress. My enthusiasm must have been contagious because Carolee would stand up in the packsack, hang on to the uprights and squeal as the "cats" pushed a big load over the side.

123

That fill, at the time it was completed, had the status of being the largest land fill in the Pacific Northwest. There were a few extra unplanned yards in it also.

Joe Orazio was running his D-8 on the west side of this tremendous heap of dirt when, suddenly, he and half of the fill were tobogganing down the hillside. With presence of mind and a strong will to survive he turned the "cat" down the hill, socked the blade down and rode his many-thousand-yard steed until it came to a halt. By the time the rest of the crew missed Joe and saw the gap in the fill, he had turned the "cat" around, and with the black smoke rolling was headed back up the unstable steep, shifty incline.

Homer was really coming to life with all of this activity. The first local bar, the Yah Shure, was doing a good business. It was owned by Ray and Shirley Lentz and their partner Hank Anderson. Ronnie and Bernie Stricke had opened the Husky bar located about where the bowling alley sets now. They had built it for a garage but decided that it would do better financially as a bar with a lot less knuckle busting.

One of the bad things that had happened with the coming of the bars was they did not have the old community dances anymore. In fact, the Women's Club sold the building to Jack and Ethyl Scott for the first local bakery. Instead, everyone would stop by the bar to get the latest news of what was happening around town. I really missed the dances and I think that most people felt the same way. It was the end of one era and the beginning of a new one. Progress takes its toll.

Lloyd was still working for Alaska Road Commission. He was running the D-7 with the forward crew. They made good progress on the road and were soon setting up the second camp. This time it was at 8 Mile (later the location of Ma Simms Gusher Bar). There was a straight stretch at 10 Mile that was long enough to land small aircraft. Several of the cat-skinners owned their own planes, so that stretch was made a little wider to give them a tie-down area and it became the 8 Mile airport.

Across from the 10 Mile tie-down area was a twenty-man squad tent belonging to Rowena and Dick Tobias, who were the cooks at 8 Mile camp. We made arrangements to stay in it while we built a wanigan. It would be our summer

home while the road was under construction. The tent was 16 by 16 with a dirt floor, except in front of the drain board and stove, where there was plywood. It had a big army surplus oil range to cook on that guzzled oil like it was going out of style.
 The design of army tents has always intrigued me. They are impossible to keep warm. There is a hole in the top that lets out any heat that might accumulate. Probably designed that way to make the guys so miserable they want to go out and fight. It affected me the same way.
 When it was finished, the wanigan was an 8 by 16 cabin on skids with a boxcar roof, a window at each end, and a side door. It was the "bush camper" of yesteryear.
 The time we spent in the tent was not terribly uncomfortable. However, when a black bear walked under the tie-down ropes on the side of tent to scratch his back, I watched the thin tent canvas bulge six inches from my face quietly, in icy fear. Please believe me when I say nobody had to encourage me the next day as I rapidly nailed up all the boards Lloyd had cut the night before in order to get that wanigan finished as fast as possible.
 One afternoon as Carolee napped I sat on the oven door of the giant government surplus oil range reading and trying to keep warm when out of the corner of my eye I saw a movement. Looking closely, I watched a rat-like head protrude from beneath the cabinet. My .22 rifle sat an arms' length away against the cabinet. I reached for it slowly. Just as I pulled the trigger that little weasel darted back under the cabinet. That is my excuse for missing at eight feet. I ran outside and tried for a second shot as he rippled across the yard, but no luck. I did get quite a bit of attention though. Carolee sat straight up in her little bed crying,"Mama, mama."
 When the men working out front on the road heard her crying they thought I had shot her accidentally and came running. I felt a little silly explaining about the huge, ferocious animal I had tried to protect myself from.
 Lloyd converted a wood-burning stove to an oil burner by taking the grates out and installing a truck piston as a fire pot. The table dropped down on hinges from the front of the cupboard and went back up to be the cupboard door when not in use. He built a cabinet across one end of the little building and installed a small sink that has a hose attached to the

drain. The hose was stretched out across the yard to a little hole that we dug and filled with gravel. Good idea, but the bears thought it looked like bologna and when they got through checking it was more like a seep hose. Across the other end, Lloyd put a built-in bed and small closet, with Carolee's bunk on the wall over the foot of the bed.

Once the wanigan was finished, Carolee and I walked, picked berries, and fought mosquitoes. One sunny afternoon I was strolling along the airstrip, with Carolee lagging behind a bit. She was contentedly talking to herself. It suddenly dawned on me what she was saying.

"'Ticks for the 'tove, 'ticks for the 'tove."

I turned around, and sure enough, she was gathering firewood. A whole armful of grade stakes the survey crew had placed there to instruct the crew how much to cut or fill. Poor baby, she was really deflated when I took them, and put them back into the little holes — hopefully the ones that they came out of. I guess it turned out all right because it is still the only straight and level part of the road from Homer to Anchor Point. Maybe they should have put her on steady.

Carolee and I occasionally walked to camp about a mile away to hear the news. On one of these jaunts, we were surprised to see a "cat" pulling a bunkhouse tent out of the woods and back in line with the others.

"How'd that get clear out in the woods?" I asked one of the men.

"Well, when Wild Bill got home about 2 a.m. from a recreational visit to town, happily singing, someone in that other tent complained. He felt that was very unreasonable and started up the 'cat' and put the man and his tent where he wouldn't be bothered while Bill finished his song."

I'm really not sure if that name, "Wild Bill," came before, or as a result of, that night.

The wanigan, our "bush camper," was finished by late July of 1948, and not a day too soon. It was time to make the move to Anchor River. The whole procession of camp cabins and tent houses on skids were pulled by the "cats." Lloyd was pulling the Catlege wanigan when he hooked onto ours.

Lucille Catlege was riding in their wanigan and called out for Carolee and me to come ride with her. The move was uneventful except when a rock, hidden in the sloppy mud, caught the floor joist, and started to tear the floor to pieces. That caused us a few minutes of concern before it dislodged without major damage.

Lloyd pulled our wanigan to the bank of the Anchor River, where we had easy access to good water. We were still washing on a scrub board, but now the water supply was handy. Such luxury. See how little it takes to make you happy when you don't have much?

I put a little pulley up over the stove and hoisted the sourdough crock up into the warm area just beneath the roof. I made a spice rack by nailing pieces of 2 by 4 between the studs above my drain board. It took about 20 minutes each day to do the house work, then, with my .22 rifle and daughter Carolee by the hand, we were off to get a spruce hen or rabbit for our evening meal. Sometimes we'd stop for a visit with Lucille. It was nice to have another woman close to visit.

The Anchor Point people invited us to their activities. We walked down the trail along the river about a half mile to Peterson's to a party and had a wonderful time. Inez Clendenen, whose husband, Larry, was working on the bridge across Anchor River, invited me to go to Homemaker's meeting at Vi and Sherm Chapman's place across the river. She stopped by on her way and we took our kids and potluck casseroles and walked across the river on a log because there wasn't any bridge yet. I have fond memories of my stay at Anchor River camp.

I was very pregnant now. I was not used to having any limitations and sat on the river bank and cried when I couldn't pull a full 5-gallon bucket up the river bank. When common sense came to my rescue, I dried my tears, emptied half of the water and pulled the half-full 5-gallon buckets up the bank. Then, one at a time, I carried them back to the cabin.

The bridge work was progressing nicely. The road from Anchor Point to Homer was improving daily. One day the foreman called to me, "Wilma, do you want to ride down with the truck driver and bring your pickup to Anchor Point?"

Exciting day to be able to drive all the way to Anchor Point from Homer. The first time I drove that stretch of road was mid-November of 1948. I can't say it was a smooth ride, but who cared. Now, I could go for groceries without having to beg a ride on the Alaska Road Commission's "cats" and trucks.

On December 5, 1948, we broke camp and went home to Homer. It was so nice to have room to rattle around instead of being condensed in the wanigan. We splurged and bought a radio. Carolee couldn't understand how it worked. When I heard her talking in the other room I went to check on her. She had her face up to the speaker saying, "You get out here. I can see you in there."

It took awhile to convince her that little talking people didn't live in that box.

I got a letter from Gram. She had cancer of the stomach with no hope of recovery. It was heartbreaking. I was never able to see her again. She spent her last days in Aunt Millie and Uncle Bill's tender care and was buried in the little cemetery at Dallas beside my grandpa, my mother and little brother.

My days were filled with sewing for Carolee and the soon-to-be-with-us baby, and hauling water from my dad's house. Carolee would sit in a box on the sled, with blankets around her and a hot-water bottle tucked next to her to keep her warm. When the weather was not so cold she would stand on the back of the sled holding onto the can of water and kick along to help push.

Christmas was always fun. There was a tree at the school with Santa giving out a stocking full of candy and oranges and apples to each child. The Women's Club assisted Santa financially. Carolee thought that was great fun. She hoarded her goodie supply and enjoyed it for a month afterwards.

On Christmas day we had dinner at Lydia and Daddy's. It was a wonderful time. Lydia knitted a bright green sweater with little snowmen on the front for Carolee. Green was her favorite color. We always had real trees to decorate in those days and started out weeks ahead selecting the tree but not taking it in until about the 20th of December.

Chapter 17

A New Baby!

In the later part of January I made plans to go to Seldovia for the delivery of my baby. Rass, one of the cat-skinners from camp, offered to fly me over in his plane. That sounded good to me. I would not have to take a two-hour boat ride, and anything that kept me from having to climb down that miserable ladder from the dock to the boat was a welcome development.

Lloyd would fend for himself and Carolee was only too happy to stay with Grandma Lydia. On the morning of the 26th, Rass and I left for Seldovia, although it had snowed in the night. I was already cutting time pretty close. Rass made a couple of passes over the small Seldovia field looking carefully at the new snow cover then decided it was okay to land. When the skis touched down, we landed with a whoosh in nearly three feet of powdery snow. Rass was busy keeping the plane from nosing over. When I stepped out I was in snow clear up to my fanny. Hmmm! Rass looked at me questioningly. I laughed and said,

"We've got it to do. Let's go."

Rass was nervous about this situation. He was very shy as he had been raised alone in the woods with his father and, although he was very intelligent, carrying on a conversation came hard for him. As we made our way toward the creek, I suddenly thought how totally ridiculous I looked with my fat tummy, wallowing along through the snow like a ship in heavy seas. I started to laugh. Poor Rass thought I was getting hysterical. When I explained he managed a weak smile. Arriving at the creek, we managed to cross in a skiff that was there. He offered to walk me into town but I assured him I would make it just fine. I felt like a quitter not helping him with the plane but this was a time when it just couldn't be helped. He had his work cut out for him to get that plane off the snowy field.

I walked the mile or so on through the snow to Juanita and Russ Berteson's house, where I was severely scolded by Juanita because I hadn't let her know I was coming so she could meet me. She worried my exertion would bring on early labor (as if I would mind getting that over a little early), but I experienced no ill effects from the journey. I went visiting with Juanita, crocheted some last minute things and waited.

On the 27th I stopped by the store and picked up a bottle of castor oil. I took it home and swallowed the contents with an orange juice chaser. Swallowing it was a breeze compared to trying to keep it down. I thought it might cut down the waiting time. About 10 p.m., after numerous trips to the bathroom, I was so nervous I decided to walk for awhile.

"Do you want me to walk with you?" Juanita asked with concern.

"No, I just feel nervous. I don't think I'll walk very far." I pulled my coat on and strolled into the night. By the time I walked the length of the Seldovia boardwalk I decided, since I was an amateur at this baby business, maybe I would walk up to the hospital and talk to someone. I went in, Nurse Betty Thorsness looked at me a little alarmed.

"Are you having pains?" she asked.

"Well, not exactly," I answered apologetically.

They had another lady who was already in labor but found time to check me. The doctor was ex-navy and thought just about everything women complained about, including pregnancy, was in their head. He seemed to feel I was having this baby just to annoy him when he was busy. As far as he was concerned it was very inconsiderate of me. Did that worry me? Not too much.

However, I ended up in a hospital bed and around 4 a.m. Constance Margaret arrived in this world. The Margaret was for my grandmother who had lived long enough to know this and the "Constance" because I liked it.

I had been given a spinal block and had the granddaddy of all headaches when I came to. Nevertheless, I wanted to hold Coni. I thought she was the most beautiful baby in the world, of course. I accepted her happily, even if I had ordered a boy. I looked down into her little face, and like most mothers, wished I could keep her safe from the tough old world out there forever.

After five long headaching days in the hospital, I was so glad when longtime acquaintance, Merle Smith, came to get me in his float plane. He knew I loved to fly and once we were airborne he said, "Here, let me see that baby. You fly us home." And I did. It was great to fly again.

Merle was an Adventist minister and one of the best Christians I have ever known. He lived his beliefs so well he didn't have to say much. His wonderful Christian experience is probably what gave him the courage to fly with someone who had not flown a plane for five years.

Lloyd was crazy about Coni and was on his very best behavior. He wasn't drinking much at this time, and sober, he was one of the easiest people in the world to get along with. That first month Lloyd, Carolee and I spoiled that baby rotten and as a result she wanted to be held and amused all of the time. Finally I said, "This has got to cease. I don't want her to be a spoiled little brat no one will be able to stand."

Well, I tell you that little lady had a mind of her own. When we didn't pick her up immediately, she managed to scream for a good half hour before she settled down and went to sleep. We all walked up and down the floor just out of her sight, worried sick. Thank goodness she learned quickly and there were no repeat performances. After that she was a good baby, enjoyed by the whole family, including Daddy and Lydia.

Loma and I sent pictures back and forth. Her little Sheryl Ann was four months older than Coni. She and her husband, Frank, were living in the central part of Oregon, where he worked as a logger.

In April, we went back to road camp. The road crew had taken our wanigan across the new Anchor River bridge and parked it. When we arrived the big DW-10s were making their turnaround right by it and it shook us thoroughly each time.

For the most part it wasn't a problem, but when I tried to bake it was. I mumbled about it one day as I put a cake in the oven.

"I hope those guys don't make this cake fall," I said to no one in particular.

A few minutes later, I heard one of the big rigs throw on the air. I looked around for Carolee, she was gone. I ran out, scared to death they had run over her. There was that pint-size child, hands on her hips, telling the operator to haul someplace else because it was making her mom's cake fall. He smiled when I came running. Carolee was very upset that after she had told them the problem, my cake baking didn't change the progress of the Sterling Highway.

The first part of May of 1949, we moved to Stariski camp. Carolee and I got busy making everything road ready. We set the sourdough pot down in the sink, and tied all of the cupboard doors shut, wrapped cardboard around the new gas washer and lashed it down securely to the stabilizing boards across the forward skids of the wanigan.

When the time came for the move I put Carolee's snow suit on her, wrapped Coni in an extra blanket, and climbed up on the D-7 beside Lloyd for the six-mile trip to our new location at Stariski River.

Everything went fine for the first mile. As we approached a deep gully I wondered how we would ever get across, then I noticed Benny Bowers standing by with the Hyster 8 on the other side. We stopped while one of the hands pulled the Hyster cable down the muddy bank and hooked onto us. With the cable attached securely, we plunged over the embankment. Starting up the other side at a rakish angle, with the connecting cable fiddle-string tight, I looked back to check my washer. Soupy mud boiled up within six inches of the top and I decided not to watch.

I looked down at the kids to see if they were afraid. Forget it. Both little girls slept peacefully. As we went through the Hostetter homestead, Amos and Sarah came out of their house and waved. Obviously, they were enjoying the excitement of the parade moving through their place. Shortly, we came around a bend in the road and there was Stariski camp already set up. Fred Blayden, Reenie's dad, was the cook and called to us to come and eat.

After lunch, Lloyd asked me where I would like to live. Once again I chose the river bank. Wonderful campsite! I put the clothesline rope up between the big cottonwood trees and nailed a board between two trees to scrub the blue jeans on that needed extra attention. Carolee and I dug a hole in the bank where it was protected from the sun and put in an empty gas case on its side. We removed the top and bottom from another case and scooted it back in the hole. On the front of the second box, we put a canvas curtain long enough to put a couple of rocks on the lower edge to hold it down securely. Our refrigerator was ready.

Across the river was a huge old cottonwood tree. We put up a swing for Carolee. She was proud to be able to walk across the bridge by herself, waving to me every few steps to assure me she was all right. When she called that she was coming home I would walk to meet her.

Hunting for spruce hens and ptarmigan was still a daily activity. Often we hunted our way through the woods and then walked down the beach to visit Bob, Lil and Pat, who were running the Walli fish trap. They would give us king salmon that was a welcome addition to camp diet.

Going to town for groceries was back to catching the freight sled, riding it to Anchor River, driving to Homer with the our truck, shopping, and getting back to Anchor Point in time to catch the freight sled back to camp.

Rass was running a scraper pulled behind a "cat," (more often called a "can" in the construction world) for ARC. He was just beyond Stariski River the day the cable broke. It came coiling forward and hit him on the back, raising a snake-like welt an inch high that turned a bluish color and seeped blood. It was obvious immediately he needed to see a doctor. The boss told another skinner, running a can, to make them a flat spot in the road. Then the crew dragged Rass's plane onto the improvised runway. He had been teaching Bennie Bowers to fly. Luckily Benny was skinning "cat" on the job and wasn't far away. They took off with Benny flying and Rass beside him giving instructions. Rass was back on the job the next morning, leaning forward on the "cat" seat to protect his sore back. Business as usual.

The only bad thing at Stariski camp was the aggravating mosquitoes. We fought them with smudge pots of Buack powder, bug repellent and mosquito netting and survived. I couldn't hunt because it was impossible to breathe without breathing in bugs unless there was a good breeze blowing. The skinners suffered too. We all smeared ourselves with "bug dope" but the mosquitoes happily licked it off and continued to nibble.

In a matter of two months the wheels of progress took us to Happy Valley camp on Rex Hanks' place. I missed the river, but settled for digging clams just over the hill. I put a five-gallon gas can with the top cut out into the bag on the pack board. Then, wrapping Coni in her blanket, I would put her in it. Taking my clam gun (shovel), a burlap sack, and with a firm grip on Carolee's little hand, we would head for the beach. If I let go of her she would run far ahead, stamping to make the clams squirt then shouting "Get this one, Mom!" When we had a half sack of clams I would switch, putting the clams in the pack board and carrying Coni home in my arms.

The clams were huge. I measured one. It was 18 inches from the end of the neck to the end of the shell, and that one clam filled a quart jar. This isn't a fish story. It's a clam story and the gospel truth.

The road work was progressing faster now as the country wasn't as swampy. Soon we moved on to Wayne Jones' camp on his homestead about five miles south of Ninilchik. The wanigans all were parked near a little stream. Wayne had a rope ladder hanging over the 50-foot bluff that we used daily to go to the beach. It was a little tricky with the kids but where there is a will there is a way. With Coni on my back in the packboard, I would go down about three steps, then Carolee would start down, and we would coordinate our stepping, with me being behind her if she slipped. She took good care of me, saying, "Tep now, tep mommie" as we descended or ascended the ladder. Coni gurgled and cooed, perfectly happy with the arrangement.

The blueberry picking was good at Wayne's. He always aimed us in the right direction, warning us not to go too far and be sure and watch for four-legged competition for the berries. I took this advice very seriously, because I had no intention of trying to climb a tree with the baby on the packboard and Carolee ahead saying "Tep, mommie."

It was at this camp, when the wind was right, the skinners began to hear the sounds of the equipment working on the right-of-way from the Soldotna end. The excitement built each day as we waited for the day when the two crews would meet and the basic final link to the outside world would be forged. We all cheered when that day came in the summer of '49, but even after all of the waiting and excitement I don't remember the date.

The medical boat, *Hygiene* was coming into Homer on its annual trip and the kids needed to get their shots. The new camp cook offered to fly us into Homer in his Piper Cub. The "cans" gave us a flat runway, but it was short because they were putting in a culvert on the straightaway where the airplanes usually took off. To make up for the short runway, several of the culvert crew hung onto the tail until the plane was shuddering. When they let go, we traveled full speed down the two-bits worth of runway. At the end of it, we dove off the roadway and banked down the creek bed and over the bluff above the beach. It was a fight between gravity and air speed; to crash or fly. Those little Cubs are great. We climbed up a thousand feet or so and followed the beach in.

It made me nervous that the door on my side of the plane had a bad latch, allowing it to flap in the breeze. I didn't realize how uneasy it made me until Carolee, who was sitting in front of me on the seat between my legs said in a pathetic little voice, "Mom, you are squishing me."

I had locked my feet around her to hang onto her as I had the baby in my arms, and the poor child was being crushed. Coni cuddled snugly on my left arm and slept placidly throughout the whole ordeal.

In the fall of 1949, I was able to bring our old International pickup to camp, load up, and head home. Carolee holding the sourdough pot and me holding Coni on my left arm, I drove the 35 miles to Homer. It was September and the road wasn't much to brag about but it was passable.

When it froze that winter, ARC ran a grader over it and people started making the journey to Seward and Anchorage. We didn't try it until January 1950. Lloyd and I bundled up the kids and prepared for the trip. In those days, with practically nothing between Homer and Seward, a person needed to prepare for any emergency that might take place. We put in extra blankets to keep us warm in case of breakdown. Something to eat: sandwiches, thermos bottles of coffee and tea, and several cans of milk. The normal road things: tire pump, chains, six quarts of oil and two five-gallon jerry cans full of gas. Oh yes, and don't forget the Fels Naptha soap to stop leaks in the gas tank temporarily. Lloyd gassed up the old International pickup and we were off on our first road trip to the outside world....Seward.

The trip going over was sunny and beautiful. The road had been graded and snow filled the holes. Lloyd was actually quite talkative, saying, "This is the spot we almost lost the D-8. We had to cut down trees and tie them to the tracks to finally crawl out of that one," and, "Oh, here's the place that it took me a whole day to get a darn big tree down. When I finally got it down I had plowed up about a half acre."

In Seward, we stayed overnight in the hotel and ate in the restaurant, a real treat. Carolee thought it was funny when I made Coni a bed in the dresser drawer and set it by the bed.

When we awoke the next morning it was to a very different situation. It was snowing! Big fat lazy flakes. The kind that can put several feet of snow on the ground in a short time. I didn't get to shop much. Just filled up the thermoses, got a loaf of bread and some lunch meat and we started back. The snow worsened as we got beyond Moose Pass. Where was that turnoff to the western Kenai Peninsula?

The engine was giving us trouble. It coughed, spluttered, and threatened to quit entirely. Lloyd stopped time and again, checking the sediment bulb and adding alcohol to the gas to keep any moisture from freezing in the gas line. Passing what we thought was a logging road Lloyd asked, "Is that our turnoff?"

"Oh, I don't think so," I answered.

And on we went through the gathering darkness. There were no signs at all. The road seemed endless. Straining our eyes through the blinding snow storm we searched for the turnoff.

Eventually we found a house that we could stop and ask where we were. It was the closest I have ever come to seeing the little town of Hope. It was 25 miles back to our turnoff and it was already dark.

The problem with the pickup seemed to be the fuel pump. When we got turned around, Lloyd lashed one of the five-gallon gas cans to the top of the pickup, pulled the gas line loose from the tank and put it into the can. This seemed to remedy the engine problems. After a tiring, bumpy ride back down the road we finally found the right turnoff.

Before we got to Hinton's Lodge we were bucking into snow drifts that sent snow flying over the cab. Every once in awhile we could see the road. Time to bunch it. We pulled into Hinton's Lodge and felt lucky to get a cabin, as we weren't the only stranded travelers that night.

Next morning, it was sunny but there was three feet of snow on the road. Like the rest of the travelers, we were anxious to get home, but it only took about a mile down the road to convince all of us there are times you have to be patient and wait for the snow plow.

It was shortly before noon when the rumbling noise of the snow plow bumping along the gravel road came to our ears. That sent us all scurrying to our vehicles and down the freshly plowed road home.

We were just north of Ninilchik. The moon was shining brightly when suddenly the right rear side of the truck dropped down. Lloyd was having a terrible time keeping the truck on the icy road. He finally got it stopped, jumped out, and discovered the axle had broken and we had lost the right rear set of dual wheels entirely. It was well below zero. There was no way we would have gas enough to keep the heater going to keep us from freezing until morning so we started walking down the hill. We had walked about half a mile when we saw the lights of Ninilchik village.

Carolee, who had remained awake, trotted along holding tightly to my hand. She acted as though all of this was done to amuse her and loved every minute. Lloyd carried Coni, and soon we were having wonderful hot tea at Mr. Jackinski's store. I looked at his thermometer and it said 32 degrees below zero. Some kind soul took pity on us and offered to drive us home to Homer. The first trip for us over the new road was at last ended.

Chapter 18

On The Road

I flew to Walla Walla in the spring 1950 to have my second baby taking Coni with me. I wore my mukluks out and created quite a sensation. My aunt and uncle were raising mint south of Walla Walla and I stayed with them.

Merlie gave a baby shower for me and it was such fun to see old friends. Loma came up from Oregon and brought her little girl, Sheryl.

Thomas Lloyd was born on the 8th day of April in the Sanitarium at Walla Walla. He was a doll. A very beautiful lifelong relationship started that day. He was my son and my friend.

He was only a week old when we left Walla Walla for Homer. Reenie and her husband, Phil, met us in Seattle and took us from Boeing Field to SeaTac for our seven-hour flight to Anchorage.

Lloyd was already out at Ninilchik at camp. They had moved the wanigan there. He urged me to "stop fooling around," and get out there.

The road was impassable due to spring breakup so Daddy offered to take the kids and me out on his fishing boat, the *Wilomalee*. We came into the Ninilchik River at the top of an 18-foot tide and Lloyd was standing by with the D-6 and sled to take us and our supplies up the hill. Coni, Tommy and Carolee weathered the trip well. As for me I was still a little weak and weary, but there was so much to do I couldn't take time to recuperate.

The road camp was set up on top of the hill. I had barely put the last of the grocery supplies on the shelves when a message came from ARC headquarters that no family could be in the camp compound, so it was pack up and move. About a mile back down the road toward Homer we found a nice campsite near a good spring and settled in.

During the winter of '49-'50 Lloyd's mother died, leaving her nine-year-old son, Halby. He had stayed with us before and we were glad to have him with us again. He was at camp with Lloyd when I got home.

Another member had been added to our family in my absence. Lloyd had gotten Halby a puppy. The pup was black Lab and springer and they had named him Blackie, for obvious reasons. With my arrival, he attached himself to me. He loved the kids, and was very tolerant as Coni crawled over him. Carolee would hug him till his eyes bulged, and he offered neither growl nor teeth. He ran and fetched for Halby Dean, but it was my feet that he lay across while I darned socks or mended kids' clothes. When I awoke in the morning and dropped my hand over the side of the bed, Blackie would give my hand a reassuring lick with his big wet tongue. Still, after many years without him, in those first moments of morning, I find myself dropping my hand over the bedside feeling for my friend.

If anything happened in the night, he wouldn't bark and wake the household. Instead he would come to my bedside and quietly lay his head on my pillow by my ear then growl softly until I checked the situation. No amount of pleading would get me off the hook until I actually looked. Only then could we both settle down. After that he would lie down breathing the equivalent of a dog sigh in a tone that said "Oh, what I have to put up with," and go back to sleep.

If any stranger came around the kids in the yard, that big friendly dog body would tense and his white teeth would show. Nobody ever pushed the issue, so I don't know if he would have actually eaten them alive as he threatened.

With the camp being near a village, Lloyd stepped up his drinking. If he got a case of beer, he quickly drank a case of beer. I got in the habit of slipping a bottle out, and dropping it in the flour bin or some other hiding place to keep him from drinking himself into oblivion. I did not have the sourdough pot anymore. Instead, I made what I always called my "Cheatin' Sourdoughs" from beer and Krusteaz. It used up some of the beer, and they tasted great. Like sourdough but lighter.

The International pickup that had carried us over so many of the rough roads finally bit the dust. We found a one-ton military vehicle that had four-wheel drive. This particular model was a big pickup with no doors and about three feet up to the running board. It went through or over anything and with road conditions being what they were, it really filled the bill.

It was good, however, that I was a blue-jeans girl as there was no ladylike way to climb into that beast without a ladder. To shift smoothly you had to double clutch. Thank goodness, I had learned that on the old Chevy truck back in the orchard days. We named the truck "Griswold," after those tough, enduring old cast-iron skillets.

I loved that truck. It was a keeper. With a little patience on my part it would see me through anything. I drove through muck and mire and was never stuck. It did on one occasion spring a leak in the radiator hose, on a lonely stretch of road, when all I had to fill it with was Tommy's eight-ounce baby bottle. After a couple of dozen trips up and down the hill and taping the hole with two whole rolls of black tape I ran the truck down the hill, filled it up at the stream and headed on home.

Going to Sunday School was an adventure. Halby and Carolee would sit on the seat. I would put Tommy's bassinet on the back of the truck right behind the cab and give Coni to Halby to hold so that I could climb in. (I had to wear a swing skirt to make the climb.) Then I would start up the truck, retrieve Coni, hold her with my left arm, and off we would go. It is no wonder she is a good driver. She grew up under the wheel.

Our last year at camp was 1950. When the main part of the actual building of the road was finished there was no longer a need for camps. ARC kept as many locals employed as possible. Lloyd worked on the road, but the kids and I stayed in Homer.

When he didn't drink, things went well. Sober, he was a patient man, a good mechanic and an excellent skinner. He was not talkative. If he talked at all, it was about mechanical things. Thank goodness I liked mechanical things.

The next two years we spent in Homer as Lloyd helped finish the road. I was in Washington at my aunt and uncle's when Carmen Suzette was born on January 4, 1952. She was a tiny thing, with big green eyes. From the very beginning she looked everyone over, as if she was carefully evaluating them.

Lloyd came out to the "States" when the season was over and we decided to stay Outside for the winter. He went to work on a farm at Prescott, about 15 miles west of Walla Walla. He liked the farmer he worked for and, outside of long hours and low wages, his job went well.

The first week after we moved into a little rented house in Prescott, Coni came down with chicken pox. Keeping food in the house became an immediate problem. Lloyd's long hours of farm work made it impossible for him to go to the store for me. Halby Dean was in school, and I couldn't leave the little ones alone. They got sick one at a time. Just when one of them was well enough for me to take them to the store with me, the next one broke out. When I thought it was finally over, Halby came down with it. That poor child was sicker than all the rest. Lloyd had to ask for time off to get groceries, and we weathered the storm.

I bought 50 baby chicks that spring to raise for fryers and planted a garden.

Two Singer sewing machine salesmen knocked on the door one day. I invited them in and served them coffee. They told me later it was not the usual reception. They did their sales pitch, and then I said, "I am really sorry, but feeding a family the size of ours on a small paycheck there's nothing left over."

"Why don't you pick out the machine you like the best and keep it for two weeks. We'll be back and see what you've decided," said the salesman. I smiled but said, "I have to tell you up front I will mend everything, and sew like mad for two weeks, because I can't afford to keep it."

They said fine, and left me a top-of-the-line Singer in a beautiful desk-type cabinet. True to my word, I sewed like mad, mending, making much needed pot holders and a quilt. I mended every little pair of jeans, sewing far into the night. The two weeks flew by and the salesmen were back. I stopped cutting up fryers, and invited them in.

"Come in and have some coffee while I take the things out of the drawers." I kept thinking how much I needed that sewing machine. Cautiously I asked, "How much would just the 'head' in a carrying case be?"

One of the fellows did some figuring on a little pad, then said "$169, $22 down and $8 per month."

"I could maybe manage the payments, but I don't have the $22 for the down payment," I admitted.

They looked at each other a minute.

"How about us taking fryers for the down payment?"

"Deal," I said happily and started packaging fryers.

Lloyd stayed on the farm job several months, working 10 to 12 hours a day for $225 a month. It was hand to mouth and it was obvious we would have to figure out something else. The Hanford Atomic project was hiring at Richland. Over the phone I found a place to rent in Kennewick that allowed kids and animals and was in easy driving distance of Hanford. Armed with Lloyd's last meager paycheck and towing a trailer loaded with our belongings, we made the move.

I was awakened the next morning by Lloyd's moans. He was in terrible pain. His genitals were swollen twice their normal size. I dressed the children quickly, and with Halby's help got Lloyd into the car. I needed to find a doctor and I didn't have any idea where to look. Looking around at the nearby houses, trying to find someone to ask, I chose a big old farm house that sat in a clump of trees just across the field below us.

"Could you tell me where I could find a good doctor?" I asked the little gray-haired lady who answered the door.

I felt I had come to the right place when Mrs. Beale told me she had been a nurse for many years. She quickly wrote down a doctor's name and instructions how to get there. In a little over an hour Lloyd was on the operating table for a strangulated hernia.

I had more worries than Lloyd being in the hospital. The few dollars we had were not going to take care of lights and phone bills or feed us for long. It was time for emergency measures. I spent a few of the precious dollars sending a wire to a man in Homer who had inquired about buying my lot in Homer. I didn't want to sell it, but when push comes to shove you gotta do what you gotta do.

Now what to do for the long haul until Lloyd could go to work? The $265 from the lot would pay rent and lights for awhile but not long, even in those days. Grapes were in season and I tried picking them. What a hopeless adventure. Lloyd was really too weak to leave alone. Taking the kids with me wasn't a good answer. They ate so many grapes they got stomachaches and kept me up all night. I couldn't make enough money to take them to a sitter.

Well, I reasoned, if it cost so much to have kids taken care of, obviously, that is what I should be doing. I put an ad in the paper.

The answers were immediate, resulting in four more little people in my household. The first couple of days were pretty bad, as I mistakenly thought I could get something done and care for eight kids. Forget that!

The third day, I got up at 5 a.m., did the housework, fixed food that took only reheating, washed and hung the clothes, bathed and dressed my babies, and was ready by 7:30 a.m. for the extra children. It was fun. We played and took walks around the place. I read to them and sometimes made up stories to tell them.

I don't remember exactly how much money I made, but it kept the lights on and fed us until Lloyd went back to work. By the time I quit doing it, I had nineteen children including my own. I wonder if that had anything to do with Lloyd's speedy recovery. Perhaps it was self-defense that sent him out to the Hanford Atomic project.

Hanford was in the very initial stages and Lloyd's "cat skinning" experience got him an immediate job. The first few days running a D-8 over rocky terrain were pitifully painful, but he persisted.

After Lloyd went back to work, I still felt I should do something to help, as we had the doctor bills to pay on top of average expenses. There was a 225-foot building on the place that was designed to raise fryers. Hmmm, why not? I talked to the people at the feed store and they sent me to a packing plant. I got a contract with the plant to take 1,200 fryers at six weeks of age, so I purchased 400 chicks a week for three weeks.

All went well until the first 400 were five weeks old and I went to check out the delivery procedure. The place was locked up tight. Surprise! The packing plant had gone bankrupt! My heart did cartwheels as I thought about the ever increasing amount of feed those chickens were eating. I have always been a little suspicious that the place I bought the feed and chicks from might have been instrumental in walking me down that garden path.

"Well, Wilma," I said to myself, "You got yourself into this, get yourself out."

As I pondered this problem, a salesman came along selling deep freezes. With my previous experience with chicken bartering on the sewing machine I was now a more seasoned barterer and in this case I certainly had plenty of bartering material. After serving him several cups of coffee I ended up with a 22-cubic foot freezer that I needed very badly and he had a twenty-chicken down payment.

Now I had a way to stop some of those chickens from eating, but a lot of chicken butchering lay ahead. There was a commercial chicken-picker stored in the processing room of the chicken building which I knew absolutely nothing about operating. In the face of the present crisis I scrubbed it with Purex water and tried to figure out how it worked. The chickens had to be killed, scalded to loosen the feathers, picked, singed to take the hair off and butchered.

The kids followed me around as I strung up a wire from the chicken building to a pole about 20 feet away. I made an outdoor stove out of a barrel and put a tub of water on to boil to scald the chickens with. I decided to do them ten at a time so I hung them up by their feet on the wire. Armed with a linoleum knife, like I had seen my uncle use in turkey harvest, I got that part taken care of.

I took the first chicken and doused it in the boiling water. So far, so good. Now for this strange machine. I'll not bore you with the details of feathers flying into my hair and on the walls but by the time I got the first ten chickens picked I had a pretty good idea how it worked. About four flops on that picker, and that chicken was naked. Greatest thing since the round wheel. Full speed ahead, I proceeded to process my chicken crop.

My plan was to fill the freezer, then look for a market. When it was full I went on to phase two. Where to start? I was a little nervous about the big restaurants that would want a contract, so I went along the truck route to the restaurants. Most of these places were in the negro section where I had never been before.

At the first place, I left the kids in the car and went to see the manager. Every head turned toward me as I walked into the place. I had never felt quite so white in my life. The lady in charge was out but returning momentarily so I waited. Soon a smiling, rather heavy-set lady came in. She looked at me, laughing, and said, "You must be the mommie who peeled the chickens."

That would be my children helping with a sales pitch. She ordered twenty to thirty fryers a week as a base order and said she would call if she needed more. Mentally armed with this success, I soon had similar orders from a dozen places.

Thank God it was in the days before quite so much legal red tape. Today it would take six months, 15 pounds of paperwork and $15,000 of improvements. I would have gone down the financial tube. This is called progress? As it was then, all went well. I didn't make any money and I was not tempted to continue chicken farming, but I did break even, unless there is a price on mental anguish.

Chapter 19

Home Again

Lloyd and I were missing Alaska terribly. He promised he could now handle the alcohol situation and we headed for home in August of 1953. Lloyd went to work on construction. We still had the house.

I was pregnant, very tired, and run down. The doctor situation in Homer was still hit and miss, so in January I went to Anchorage for the delivery. My cousin, Harry Barnum Jr., was in Anchorage, and he and his wife invited me to stay with them until the baby arrived.

Harry is a good cook and a very caring person. He made big fluffy slices of French toast, and tied my mukluks for me. I was so grateful, it was hard to keep from crying. I have always said that if Harry and his wife hadn't taken such good care of me those last two weeks I wouldn't have had the strength to have that child.

Tamara Louise was born January 18, 1954, at the old Providence Hospital. I had been in Anchorage for two weeks before I went to the hospital. Lloyd was cross with me for taking so long and called the hospital with the old "stop fooling around" routine. I got up out of bed and left the hospital. I was home when Tam was 24 hours old, against the doctor's wishes, I might add, but I didn't have to live with the doctor.

There were a few minutes at the airport when I looked up that long stairway and wondered if I could make it. I lucked out. Yule Kilcher breezed up alongside of me saying, "Here, give me that baby." Then he put a helping arm around me, and we flew up those steps. I don't think I have ever told him that I could never have made it without him.

I have heard some young mothers complain about caring for a bunch of kids. No matter how tough things got, I never felt that way. The kids and I had so many wonderful times.

Halby was good about getting in the coal and doing his homework for school. The little ones played school in the living room, using gas cases for seats and desks. Coni was the teacher and ruled with a firm hand. When someone visited they would say, "Wilma, how do you keep your sanity with all of these kids?"

What problem could they possibly be referring to?

The kids' favorite stories were Longfellow's "Hiawatha" and poems out of the old poetry book that had been my mothers. Like me, they loved Robert Service's "Cremation of Sam McGee" and "Dangerous Dan McGrew." I always thought it was the melodious rhythm of Longfellow's works that made it appealing to the children, because I don't think the words made much sense to them at that young age. Tommy had his own way of enjoying it — about five minutes and he was asleep.

Lloyd had a chance to go back to work for the ARC steady if we would move to Kenai. Tammy was three months old when we moved to a very cold log cabin several miles from Kenai with no neighbors close. My memories of that place are cold, and difficult. I washed clothes in a gas washer, hanging them outside to freeze dry by snapping them out straight and pinching them to the line in the -50 degree temperature. Jeans and sweaters hung on a rack by the stove because they took so long to freeze dry, making the house like a banya with the steam freezing on the windowpanes.

The car had to have the headbolt heater plugged in whenever it was not in use, and you would think you were riding a bucking bronco when you started to drive it anywhere as the tires would be frozen flat on one side. It galloped down the road, ker-whumpty-whump, until the frozen tires got round again.

The children couldn't play outdoors as they were too little to realize the freezing dangers that could creep up on them so quickly. They pressed their noses to the windowpane like little caged animals. I spent as much time as I could entertaining them. I read to them and I made up stories using their names, which delighted them. The spare moments, I spent sewing clothes for the kids on my beloved Singer sewing machine.

When the cabin owners returned we had to move. We rented what used to be the teacher's quarters, upstairs in the old school in downtown Kenai. Its good points were a big hallway where the kids rode their tricycles, other children for them to play with, and sometimes there were movies downstairs in the old classrooms. Also I could take the children to Sunday school and visit with people.

The bad points were no running water, as the downstairs wasn't kept heated and the pipes would freeze. We had to haul snow in buckets up the outside stairs and melt it in a tub on the stove for general use such as washing dishes and bathing. We hauled our drinking water from Pappy Walker's place several miles away in five-gallon jerry cans.

I really didn't mind hauling the water as it gave me a chance to visit with Pappy Walker and his wife, Mandy. The worst thing by far was a bar a couple of blocks away. The living conditions were bearable, but I was sick when Lloyd started drinking again.

It was hard to be happy and get through the cold winter days. I was at the end of my rope. I got to the place where I could sit down and stare out the window and mentally lose myself in a warm sunny world where everyone was laughing. I would suddenly realize one of the kids were shaking me and shouting. I had just enough sense left to know I was losing it.

The climax hit one night when Lloyd came home really drunk. I was sewing and it seemed to infuriate him. The six-cell flashlight was laying on the kitchen drain board. He grasped it firmly and, before I could get out of the way, hit me over the head with it.

When I came to I was shivering, laying in a pool of blood and he was sleeping soundly. Halby was awake and very frightened. He helped me get up and get the babies dressed.

I gathered a few immediate necessities and we quietly tiptoed down the stairs. I got things loaded and everybody settled in the car before I crept back upstairs for the keys that were in Lloyd's pants pocket by the bed. I didn't know what he would do if he realized I was leaving. I didn't breathe as I took the keys and quietly hurried down the stairs, jumped into the car, locked the doors and prayed the car would start in the frigid below-zero weather. I turned the starter. Umm Umm Umm, it ground. My heart was pounding, my head was splitting, and the blood was running off my chin. I pumped the gas pedal. Suddenly the motor came to life, just as Lloyd came running down the stairs and tried to jerk the car door open. The kids were crying. I wheeled away with tires spinning.

I went to my nurse friend, Mandy Walker, as the blood kept running into my eyes and made it hard to see when I drove. She fussed and stewed as she shaved the damaged area on my head. It took 18 butterfly tapes to hold my wound together.

"I hope that you have learned your lesson," she scolded. "You should have gone long ago." Then she gave me a hug. What a wonderful lady. Her bandages held and got me home to Homer.

The Homer house was rented to the Everns family and I didn't know just what we were going to do. I guess I had just underestimated Alice Everns. She just said, "Come in, dear. Our house is nearly ready and in the meantime we will just scoot over." I couldn't help crying like a big baby. She let me cry on her shoulder for a few minutes and then said, "Now let's get you settled." We shoved the two big beds together upstairs and the kids and I all curled up together. Alice gave me two pills for my headache and we all went to sleep.

I had little money. It was obvious we had to do something about that. The ever faithful "Griswold" was still in running order and when a good southwest wind came, the kids and I went to the beach and hauled coal. Some went to Alice's place to help make it right for the groceries we were eating and her keeping the littlest ones while the rest of us were on the beach. We got coal in for us and sold some to get gas and groceries. In those days, there were no safe houses or easily acquired dollars. It was a matter of figuring things out for yourself.

Everns' house was finished soon and we helped them move. Daddy brought us a sack of potatoes from his root cellar that helped a lot. I made potato soup, scalloped potatoes, fried potatoes, and we all ate. Halby went back to school and I did all of the things that mothers with a house full of kids do. My head was healing.

About three o'clock one morning I woke up to find Lloyd in the house. I tried to be calm, and went into the living room to talk to him. His first question was, "Are you ready to behave yourself and come home or do I have to see to it that you do?"

He didn't ask if my head was better, or how we had been managing to survive.

"Lloyd, the kids, and I are managing. I have no desire to go back," I said, much more calmly than I felt.

"Well, I had hoped that you would not force me to burn the house down but now I must."

I had been pacing the floor, my back was to him, when he said that. I turned around slowly, trying to comprehend what he was saying. He had his cigarette lighter lit, and was holding the flame under the paper drapes. Thank the good Lord they were fireproof. I tried not to show fear, because it might send him into a rampage. I moved casually toward the area of the front door, saying something idiotic like, "O shoot, a nice bonfire, and I don't have any marshmallows."

When I was even with the door I jerked it open and bailed out. We had never put steps up to it so I landed on the ground four feet below, running. I ran to my neighbors' houses across the street and rousted three men who came to my aid. All I asked was that they keep him under control until I could get my kids dressed and out of the house. I am grateful to those men. Especially when they stood firm when Lloyd sat casually smoking a cigarette when we came into the house, and said in a bored voice, "What kind of silly thing has she been telling you now?"

I got the kids up, dressed them, and went to my dad's place. I got a restraining order but was scared out of my mind. About a month later, he came down in the daytime and called me to come down to the cafe on the pretext he had some money for me. We needed it desperately, so I went down. He gave me the money then said, "I am going to tell you how things are going to be. I am coming back to Homer, to live at home."

"Oh no, Lloyd, I just can't go through that anymore." I felt sick.

"Oh, I think you will. Either you will or I will kill the kids one at a time." Why should I have been surprised? "I will quit drinking, too" he added.

151

Now, I don't think he would have killed them, but at that time it was a chance I felt I couldn't take. With me frightened out of my mind, we started into the final stretch. He did quit drinking. He did come back to Homer. I walked, I talked, I moved and I prayed I could keep my sanity for the kids' sake.

Chapter 20

A Big Yellow "Cat"

In 1956 some things happened that sent me down the road of a very special experience and kept my mind busy. Yule Kilcher, the friend who helped Tammy and me up the stairs in the airport, had purchased a TD-14 International tractor. He needed an operator and Lloyd took the job. It started us in custom "cat" work. It was obvious early on that this particular arrangement was not going to work. Too many cooks working on this porridge. Lloyd ran that "cat" for about six months before he decided to look for something else.

Red Ballentine, who had worked on the road crew with Lloyd, had purchased a D-6 cat with wide-gauge pads and had been doing custom "cat" work for several years in the area. It was a blow to the community when he was killed in a plane crash in 1954.

His sister, Miriam, who had financed his "cat," came up to care for her financial investment. Miriam and her husband thought running the operation wouldn't be too complicated, but it was not working out well for them. I chatted with Miriam in the store one day and she was telling me her problems.

"Would you like to sell the 'cat'?" I asked.

"Yes." she said thoughtfully. "I think that's the only answer."

"What would you have to have for it?"

"We should get $5,000," she answered.

That evening, I asked Lloyd if he wanted Red's "cat." He looked at me like I had lost my mind.

"Do you know how you are going to pay the $15 light bill?" he asked.

"No, but I will. I have $7 toward it and I am going to give a gal a permanent and that is $5. I'll figure out something on the other $3. But that isn't what I asked you."

"Of course, I would like to have the "cat," but it is totally ridiculous. There isn't any way we could afford it."

I have always been intrigued by things people think can't be done, especially if its impossible. I had to try.

As I washed the dishes and ironed clothes, I thought about him saying it couldn't be done. Maybe he's right, but maybe I'll put on my best jeans and go down to the Homer Bank and see.

The bank was in the basement of Hewlett's house. I had never asked a bank for anything but check blanks before. When I asked Mr. Mathews if I could talk to him a minute, I was scared to death. I tried to sit up straight and look self-confident and business-like, but my voice shook.

"We need $5,000 to buy Red Ballentine's 'cat'," I stated quickly. I crossed my blue-jean clad legs so he wouldn't see my knees shaking.

"Oh, you do?" He tried not to smile, probably thinking of our $22 bank account that was going to buy groceries for the six of us for the next two weeks. His amusement spurred me on.

"Yes, sir, and I would like to get it so we could start lining up spring work."

I will always thank that man for not laughing out loud.

"What are you going to use for collateral?" he asked a little more seriously.

"How about our house? Of course we need to use it while we are paying you back."

I wasn't just sure what that "collateral" word meant, but I knew it had something to do with making him more comfortable while we had his money.

"Bring down your deed and we will take a look," he said.

"Thank you very much. I could bring it right back down."

"Tomorrow will be fine," he said firmly, trying to slow down this runaway person.

The next day, I brought the deed and ran into the first obstacle. It was made out to me in a lifetime trust and could not be mortgaged. I went home, washed dishes and cooked dinner, thinking hard. The next morning, I went to see Sam Bell, who had property behind ours.

"Sam, how would you like to have a recorded right of way from the main road to your property behind me?" Sam's eyes lit up happily. He loved property and very seldom let one foot of it go. Then he got suspicious.

"Wilma, what do you want?"

I pulled out a map I had brought along. "Look, here on this map. Do you see this little triangle, right behind my property, that doesn't even fit very well with your place? I would like to have that." After we hassled back and forth through the weekend, we made out the necessary papers.

Tuesday, Mr. Mathews opened his door, and I was the first one in. I know he thought he had gotten rid of me.

"I'm really pretty busy," he said.

"I'll talk really fast," I bargained.

"Well, all right, but just five minutes."

I pulled the deed out of my back jeans pocket. I wasn't as frightened now. I laid out the plan.

"We will knock down the hill behind the house. Put the house on skids, pull it back onto this other piece of property and you will have your collateral." He was looking at the deed from Sam in awe. I went on, "There is just one hitch. I need the 'cat' to move the house and do the leveling."

"Well, even if I agreed to the money, how would you repay it?"

"Give me ten days after we have the "cat" in our possession and I will show you a work program."

This was fun. I was beginning to see daylight at the end of the tunnel. I guessed I should say something to Lloyd.

As I served Lloyd his coffee the next morning I tried to think how to tell him so he wouldn't be upset. I set his coffee in front of him. "Well, if you've got it to do get on with it," I thought.

"Lloyd, remember when you said you'd like to have Red's 'cat'?" I launched out.

"Yeah, and remember how silly I said it was to even think about it?" he answered, sipping his coffee.

"Yes, but I had a couple of ideas and they worked, so if you'll come down to the bank with me this morning and sign papers, you could have it."

He looked at me very carefully to see if I had lost my mind. Then I explained what he would have to do.

Lloyd was a hard worker and we never missed a lick on our agreement.

I got a girl to take care of the kids, and while Lloyd knocked down the hill and put the house on skids I started laying out the first run. There were a lot of places that needed land cleared to prove up on their homesteads. There were roads to be built, yards to be landscaped. I hiked back into homesteads, talked with the people, laid out financial arrangements. It was something to concentrate on and I enjoyed the people. It was the happiest I had been in a long time. I watched Lloyd and timed the jobs until I was able to do cost estimating.

One of the first jobs we did was the pad for the first Homer Electric building. It didn't take long for us to realize we were not out of the woods yet. That poor old "cat" was in bad shape. The rails were worn so badly the tracks wanted to fall off. Lloyd would go ahead twenty feet and then back up ten to keep from losing the track before continuing.

We had spooled one-inch steel-core cable on the Hyster in order to pull out those big stumps and not have it break. The idea was great, but the cable was very heavy. When you start dragging that kind of cable the first three feet isn't bad, but from then on you have your work cut out for you. I weighed 120 pounds at the time. It took all of my muscles and a lot of grim determination to pull 30 feet of cable out and hook it onto a stump.

It brings to mind a poem I wrote about that time. It said in part, "Our swing frame is busted, our rollers are flat, we can't work on this, because we are working on that." And that surely summed up our situation.

We had no lowbed trailer to haul the "cat" with, so it had to be "walked" from one job to the next, which was hard on the already bad running gear. It was also time consuming. We got a system: Lloyd would put in ten or twelve hours on the "cat," I would drive out, give him the car to go home to eat and rest while I walked the "cat" to the next job, and he would pick me up later.

I was back-blading the yard at home one day with the D-6, pulling steering clutches around my very pregnant tummy, when my next-door neighbor, Ed King, a retired construction man motioned for me to stop. He climbed up on the track and pinned a 302 Operating Engineers button on my jacket saying, "I don't want you to get in trouble running 'cat' without your "Operating Engineers 302" button."

He laughed when I asked him if I needed a special ribbon attached, being a pregnant operating engineer.

Getting the "cat" from one job to another if it was very far was still a problem. In desperation, we bought an old Autocar truck to haul the cat on, and that miserable thing about hundred-dollared us to death. First it was carburetor, then rings, then something else. It was too high to load the "cat" on safely, but we were desperate. It was an extremely top-heavy load.

One morning the guys left with the truck and "cat" for a job on West Hill. The inevitable happened and in half an hour they were back with a wild story about going across a narrow fill with soft shoulders, and dumping everything. They assured me the "cat" was fine, took an oil change up, got the "cat" going, and pulled the truck out. They walked the "cat" on over to the job. I guess they had enough thrills for one day.

Believe me when I say life was never dull during those construction days. Each month it was a challenge to collect enough to cover our payments. With the parts orders that were flying back and forth I figured we were paying at least half of the parts crew's wages at NC Co. The serial number 9U2 5424, is indelibly imprinted on my mind from repeating it so many times. I was on a first-name basis with all of their parts men.

Lloyd and I worked out a system for Maxwell Construction. His job was to do the actual dozer work and keep the equipment greased and mechanically sound. My part was to keep work lined up ahead of the "cat," lay out the day's work and run lead car if it was needed, collect for the work, answer the phone, and if parts were urgent I better run into Anchorage and get them. It kept us both out of mischief.

Going after parts was a six-hour grind. It was still gravel roads as far as the Seward "Y." The rest was black-topped but very winding. I usually ran up in the evening, getting into Anchorage about midnight. The next morning, as soon as things opened up, I would call everybody and do the ordering. I'd give the places a few minutes to round up my orders while

I ate a bite, then run pick things up, get the car ready for the road, and try to make it back in time to fix dinner that evening.

The only bad thing was I didn't have much time with the kids and I missed that. Sometimes I would take one of my little ones with me so we could visit. Quite often it would be Carmen. She was such a little live wire I felt guilty when I left her with some poor unsuspecting baby-sitter. Also, she was completely portable. If she was tired, she disintegrated into a little heap on the front seat; awake she was interested in everything around her. There was only one road to Anchorage but she loved maps and would study them carefully. I would say, "Am I going the right way, babe?"

"Yes, you are doing fine. Just stay on this road," she would say very seriously. Good idea.

When Coni went along, she had fun preparing for the trip. It was good that I had a van with lots of space. She brought water to drink, books to read, apples and oranges to eat, and a coloring book if the trip got boring.

When it was Tomtom's turn he told me stories right out of his vivid imagination.

Little Tammy was a love bug. Lost amidst so many brothers and sisters, she treasured the time she could spend being the "only one." There wasn't anything wrong with Tammy's imagination either. One afternoon as she played with her little toy cow on wheels, she spoke to it very seriously. "I want you to watch out for those little green men because they will eat you." Then she shook her little finger at the wooden animal as it stared back blankly.

I couldn't resist commenting, "Well, I don't think I like them very well if they act like that."

A bit puzzled to find me in her make-believe world, she looked at me for a moment. Then she said, "Well...they don't like you either."

I wasn't sure if it was because I didn't taste as good as the wooden cow or my personality, but with that knowledge I have always avoided little green men.

Terrill was born in the midst of the construction activities on the 26th of May, 1956, and none of us slowed down much to welcome him. I didn't try to take him on the Anchorage trips. First, because he was too little, and then after he was six months old it was impossible to keep him in one place for five minutes. When seat belts came into being I thought of that child and was saddened by the fact someone didn't think of them sooner.

This was a truly great time in my life. My babies were such a pleasure. Lloyd was sober, and I dearly loved the construction game. We bought a backhoe, model E Quickway with a 30-foot boom, 10-foot jib and a dragline set up, and two five-yard army surplus 6-by-6 dump trucks. It rounded out our small construction company. When the weather was too wet for "cat" work, we hauled gravel.

When I had time to help, I would drive one of the trucks. We hauled off the beach, and it was a fight coming through the loose gravel loaded. I had told Jack Hendrickson, who had Prescott Equipment in Anchorage, about my problem and he called one day. "Wilma, I've got some tires like Rommel used in the desert on 18-inch rims. They should work great for you hauling gravel off of the beach down there."

I jumped into the pickup and went straight to Anchorage with checkbook in hand. I bought them for both trucks. He was right, they were made for that beach haul.

I was trying very hard to get everything paid off when the old D-6 creaked slowly to a standstill. This time, I went to NC Co. to talk to Cal Bashaw, who was running the Caterpillar department. I had more confidence now. I asked, "Cal what is a new D-6 worth?"

"We get $26,000 for a new one with the 12-foot blade, 18-inch pads and a Hyster like you need in Homer."

When we finished chatting the arrangements were made. They would give us a good trade-in for the old "cat" and the balance we would pay by the month.

They sent a man down to appraise the old "cat." He measured the poor, tired, worn-down-to-nothing grousers that had walked the "cat" down so many gravel roads on his special little grouser gage and then measured them again.

"What's the matter?" I asked.

"Oh, I was just trying to figure this out. It says 3/4 less than nothing." I guess we got our money's worth out of that "cat."

What a glorious day when that new cat rolled into the yard. No more wondering what was going to break next. It saved me hours by not having to notify everyone that we would be late getting to their job because of a breakdown. The kids were well. Things looked good.

Then one of those dark clouds showed up. Two payments short of having the "cat" paid for and four payments short of having the backhoe and trucks paid for, Lloyd fell off of the wagon. They hauled him home from the bar drunk out of his mind. I walked the floor and cried the sad miserable tears that come when there is nothing else you can do.

I begged and pleaded with him to sober up, but I might as well have talked to the wall. One morning about 5 a.m. a pickup pulled into the yard. I got up and opened the door. They dragged him from the back of the pickup, carried him inside and laid him on the floor. He had vomited all over himself and was completely dead to the world. I got a blanket and put it over him.

I sank into a chair. When would the beatings start? Would he hurt the children? Could I live with this stinking heap of humanity and keep my mind together enough to raise my kids? All of the old worries came flooding back.

I made a decision that would be final. I woke the kids as he lay on the floor, and told them to dress and pack a suitcase with their most important things. A box full of groceries, and a few pots and pans were put into the Buick wagon. Then, stepping over his inert body, we drove to our little summer cabin on a lake about eight miles out of Homer.

I was completely and totally finished. My inner feelings told me that I had done all that I was capable of. For myself and my children's sake, I must try to preserve my health, and sanity. I would do the best I could.

Chapter 21

Is There Really a Santa?

It was a muddy quarter of a mile hike into the summer cabin from the main road. There was no running water but the lake was handy. I didn't have much cash, and taking stock of the situation was a little frightening.

The good news was the kids were fine, and we had a few groceries. Somehow we would make it. It was time to get on with life, whatever it might hold. I was sure Lloyd would never help us, and from that day to this he never contributed ten cents. I collected a few outstanding bills, worked some waitress jobs, and we ate.

It didn't take long to realize I had to get back to town in order to pick up more work and for the kids' school activities. My gas bill for the car was killing me financially, and the kids were missing the afterschool fun things.

Earlier Lloyd and I had made a deal for a house out on the bluff, that had belonged to Red Ballentyne's estate. I told Lloyd I was going to move into it, and he just shrugged. I figured it was his way of saying he wouldn't give me trouble about it. I looked it over. It had a lot of bad points but at least we'd be about three miles from town, and we moved into it.

That house was a whole experience in itself. It was immediately evident there was no insulation in those walls. The windows had been poorly installed, and when a sou'wester blew, the curtains flagged happily in the breeze. This was fine in the summer but with winter's icy gales and the water freezing up in October, it was haul coal and water every day with the car. How I would have liked to have that old "Griswold" truck again. It was a discouraging time, but we had it to do, and we worked at it.

Everything I attempted to do, I ran into a brick wall. I filed for divorce but couldn't get final papers without money. I couldn't sign any papers, or do any business to make money without the divorce. It was a nightmare time.

People who could see my plight wanted to adopt my children. I knew they were trying to help, or I would have been furious. Many people took sides who didn't know the particulars. How could that nice quiet Texas boy who always said "Yes ma'am" possibly do anything bad?

Sometimes my check from the cannery was only about $20 or $30 for the week. One time in the dead of winter it was $9. I comforted myself with the thought that if I could come through these difficult times it would make me stronger. Based on that theory, I figured I should be ready to compete with Atlas by spring.

Charlie Williams, whose family had moved to Homer from Iliamna Bay several years before, moved into a cabin on the other side of Mud Bay. He would come by to visit, and bring us a rabbit he had shot or three or four spruce hens. It helped a lot, and I would invite him to stay for dinner. Then the day came he offered to pay me if he could eat two meals a day with us. I readily agreed and it saved the day.

I am sure that my guardian angel was working overtime again. Keeping groceries in the house was a constant challenge. One winter day I heard a car in the driveway. I looked out the window, and there was Charlie's friend, Alan Roehl, walking up the path with a hind quarter of moose meat on his shoulder. I was so grateful. It was freezing cold so I was able to stretch the meat over a month and save a nice roast for Christmas.

On Christmas Eve that year, we stoked the barrel heater up cherry red to get some heat in the house. It was still chilly, so we wrapped blankets around us and sat in the big chairs by the fire singing Christmas songs. The kids were really good about the fact that we wouldn't have any Christmas presents.

Suddenly the back door flew open, and with bells ringing, Santa breezed into the room, saying "Ho Ho Ho." I sat dumbfounded as he gave lovely gifts to each person: perfume, sweaters, little trucks and teddy bears. Then he gave me a hug and Ho Hoed out the back door. I can't tell you how totally surprised I was, and the kids were delirious with joy. Would you believe that I have never known who sent Santa to our house in a little town like Homer?

When the kids recovered from their shock they went out with a flashlight to find tracks. They wanted to see if he came in a sleigh, but for some strange reason the foot prints just stopped at the end of the path and the new fallen snow lay undisturbed.

The winter finally gave way to spring, and I couldn't have been happier. We still hauled coal each weekend. I waitressed at some banquets and every little bit helped. Our practice of having family meetings to work out the distribution of the few dollars we had worked great. When everyone had a say there was less complaining about what we couldn't have.

Coni and Carmen baby-sat when they could and helped buy their own clothes. Tommy did odd jobs and wanted to have a paper route but we were too far out of town for him to try that.

It was vital that I make some money that summer. Enough to catch up the house payments, and pay for my divorce. It had to be something that would let me take the kids with me. How about set-netting over on MacDonald Spit?

Chapter 22

Let's Go Fishing

Well, fishing wasn't such a bad idea if we could make it work. I started looking into what I would need, and how we would get it.

My sister, Loma, and her husband had a 13-foot skiff with a 10-horse Mercury kicker and some nets they would sell. I caught a ride to Seldovia to see Jack Lynn at the cannery. Bless his heart, he came through with the financing and I had the basics for fishing.

My brother, Sonny, was running a cannery on the spit. He had a boat, the *Artic Queen,* so he and Charlie took me across the bay to drop my moorings. They also gave me some fishing pointers. It was a beautiful day, the weather was perfect, they were both experienced fishermen, and the instructions sounded quite simple. Something like when you read the seed catalogue in the spring with the beautiful pictures in it.

School closed and we moved across the bay to Chris Spillum's old log cabin on MacDonald Spit. Early on, we met our very salty little neighbor, Sera Baxter and her Afghan hound, Sahadi. Sera gave us a lot of very good advice and was good company.

There was no water on the spit so we hauled it in the skiff from across Kasitsna Bay about half a mile. Our life took on a whole new flavor on MacDonald Spit. Our priorities were much different. Was the skiff tied up? Which way is the wind blowing? When is the tide high? Do we have enough wood to keep the house warm if we get a three-day blow? Enough water? Our financial situation was not great, but we were getting our gear paid for and eating regularly. We worked hard at keeping our grocery bill down.

Our first excursions were to dig clams. Charlie came to see us often. He built us a live box to keep our clams and Dungeness crabs in. He built us a pram, or little boat, to get out to the live box and so we could take better care of the skiff. It was only about six feet long and very cranky (tipsy) but it did the job. Now we could tie the 13-foot skiff to the live box and it wouldn't go dry or beat on the beach if a wind came up.

The first time we set gear it was under Charlie's strict supervision. We not only caught fish in our net, but the Dungeness crab were plentiful too. They were a welcome addition to our diet, but untangling their many legs from the set net is a study in patience and self-preservation. You must hold them securely by their back legs or they will show you how capable they are with those pincers. I promise you, you'll be sorry. They seem to feel they have a lot at stake, and will bite clear through your hip boots and oil skins. They also love fingers.

On wash day we would go up Jakolof Bay, taking along the wash tub, soiled clothing, five-gallon jerry jugs, our food for the day, and our .22 rifles. There is a nice little stream about a quarter of a mile inside the bay, and we set up our wash camp close to it to have lots of water available. Making a place to set the tub was done by putting two rows of large rocks about 18 inches apart. The fire was built between them and the wash tub full of water set on to heat. The smallest children would gather wood for the fire under the tub, and also a stack to take home for our wood stove. Coni would get things set up for washing, and Tom and I would take the .22s and head up Red Mountain road to get some rabbits. A nice change from our seafood diet.

When we got back from hunting, we moved the tub full of hot water off the heat and replaced it with a pan full of bay water to cook the crab we brought along. Sometimes, we barbecued salmon fillets, weaving green branches through them, and placing them on sticks over the coals.

Taking turns, we scrubbed and wrung the clothes. Tommy would fill the Jerry jugs, and put them in the skiff ready to take back to the cabin. We timed all of this operation so we could catch a fair tide back across Kasitsna Bay to the cabin. Tired, clean, happy, and weary we would sing our way home with old favorite songs such as "You Get a Line and I'll Get a Pole, Honey." When we got back to the cabin there would still be work on the net to be ready for fishing the next day.

Our grocery bill at the end of the season was only $66 for the six weeks we were there. All of us were golden brown. I am so sorry I did not get more pictures of that wonderful summer: the trips to wash, the little otter who liked to lay on the live box with his tummy turned up to the sun, the clam-digging episodes, my wonderful kids tanned and happy, Sera and Sahadi. Saying I was too busy to take pictures to preserve those memories is a poor excuse.

There were times we had problems. One of those gear pulling days, Tom and I started out at 5 a.m., allowing extra time to be sure we had all 105 fathoms of our gear pulled in time for an 8 a.m. closure. It was difficult navigating in the pea soup fog to begin with, and then, to add insult to injury, when we could see the net it was surrounded by a solid mat, a hundred feet across, of bull kelp.

Tommy and I took turns running the outboard, while the other one lay over the bow of the boat with the machete, cutting a path through the kelp to the net. When we finally got to the net we turned the outside line loose and started edging it toward the beach. We followed this procedure with each net. They were much too heavy with kelp to hope to get them into the boat. Tomtom was a good fishing partner, very serious about whatever we were doing. My one problem was keeping him from overdoing when he tried to take care of me. His little 12 year old body had its limitations.

One really nice day we were picking net on the outside of MacDonald Spit. I was picking and Tom was leaning over the side, helping to pull the net up. Suddenly he said, "Mom! We have a big fish! Maybe it is a shark or something."

I stopped picking to look. It was a king salmon, barely gilled. Looking at it down through the water it looked enormous.

"Tom, where is that gaff hook?" I asked, looking around the boat for the small hand hook that should be here. He started to look and then said, "I must have taken it out when I scrubbed the boat down."

I thought about that for a minute.

"I think if we pull him up very carefully until he just breaks the surface, we can both drive our picking hooks into the sides of his head, grab the other rail and, hopefully, pull him into the skiff. I'll keep him in the boat, and you run the boat ashore. OK?"

"Good, Mom, let's do it," Tom agreed, grabbing the net.

It worked smooth as silk, outside of me having a time keeping that fish still until we got ashore. He literally turned handsprings while I did everything but lay on him and Tommy laughed his head off. When we got that fish on the scales, we found that we had a 55 pound king salmon.

On one of our first picks we made just about all of the mistakes a person could possibly make. Coni and I were peeling potatoes when I suddenly remembered that it was time to set out. "Oh oh, set-out time. I wonder where Tom is."

"I can go with you, Mom."

"Okay." And off we went.

I called to Carmen, "We are going to set the net. Watch out for the little kids and tell Tom when he shows."

Carmen answered with an OK and we headed out, Coni running the kicker and me stacking the gear so it was ready to set out.

In a few minutes we came up on our first set just inside of Nubble Point, and I made my first mistake. We were coming up on the outside buoy. I decided it couldn't make too much difference if we just hooked onto the outside one first. Oh boy, was I ever wrong. Coni was going for the beach stern first and I was feeding the gear out over the bow. As the stack of net dwindled I looked toward the beach for my tie-off line.

Bad news! The tide was running hard, we were parallel to the beach with just a few fathoms of net showing, and the buoy was somewhere under the water, probably 10 fathoms down. When I mess up I do it big time. Now I made my second mistake. I turned the skiff around and tied a line to my submerged net, trying to tow it into shallow waters. I opened up on the throttle on the outboard motor and slurped up several fathoms of net into the propeller.

Still trying to rectify my mistake, I tipped up the motor and reached for my knife that should be in the scabbard on my belt. The scabbard was empty! We all wore hunting knives, so I turned to Coni. "Let me use your knife. I must have left mine where I was peeling potatoes." She reached for hers and, looking guilty, said, "Mom, I was helping you peel. Remember?"

We were in trouble. I sat back to evaluate the situation. At this point we were attached to an outboard motor that was attached to a net that had 20 fathoms submerged, that was attached to an engine block we were using for a mooring. Oh yes, and we were far enough out into Eldred Passage that any unsuspecting fishing boat that happened through there could wrap our net into their propeller.

I happened to look toward MacDonald Spit and there was Tommy in the "Teacup," our little pram, rowing toward us at top speed. I called to him, "Tommy, have you got a knife?"

He paused momentarily, then shouted in a disgusted tone, "Of course."

Tommy was pretty young, but he was having all of the normal male reactions. I think he even mumbled something about "dumb women should know better than go off without a knife" as he patiently cut us out of the net. If it hadn't been true I would have taken that boy to task.

Once back at the house, hungry and tired, the kids looked to me for the answer to what we would do next. I had been thinking about that. Picking up the tide book I said, "In the morning I will catch a fair tide to Homer. Perhaps Charlie will have time to get things straightened out for us."

God must have figured I had been punished enough for not obeying instructions, as the day dawned bright and clear.

I got on my boots and started for the boat. I was surprised to see Tommy filling the gas cans.

"Tomtom, I can do this. You don't have to go."

We hadn't made this trip before without Charlie. Tommy did not say that after what I had pulled yesterday there was no way he was going to trust me to make the trip alone, but the mental vibes were pretty strong.

The trip across the glassy surface of Kachemak Bay was uneventful and we found Charlie working on crab pots just up from where we beached. He had seen us coming and met us with a worried, "What's the matter?"

As soon as we had related our tale of woe he got the speed boat with the 35-horsepower motor, put the 13-foot skiff under tow and we headed back across. The really amazing part of the story is that our relationship ever went any further after he saw the hole in the net that you could have driven a jeep through, which he patiently mended mesh by mesh. I made him good things to eat and was very humble.

I did learn my lesson. I have never since ever hooked onto the outside buoy first. I never again tried to tow anything without at least 100 feet between me and the object under tow. And last but not least, Charlie forgave me...I think.

The experiences of that summer were priceless, and the healing effect it had on my mind was good. I was at peace as far as Lloyd was concerned. I finally felt I had done everything I could possibly do to make it work, and it was over. Somehow the frightening aspects of surviving from day to day I put into the category of "One day at a time, Lord." Each morning, I opened my eyes to thank the good Lord for a beautiful new day free of any worry except surviving.

By the time we went back to Homer in the fall I was able to get the divorce finalized.

Charlie was becoming an important factor in my life by then, but he was quite a bit younger than I was and I worried that no matter how I felt personally, this might not be a good working situation. We dated, had fun dancing, outings with the kids to movies, and boating excursions.

He was impulsive and would pop into the house, saying things like, "Why don't you make some sandwiches and we'll go across the bay for a picnic." At first it seemed crazy to me, but I became more tractable. He asked me to marry him, and I tried to explain to him about putting up with other people's kids on a permanent basis.

I love my kids, but they are not the shy, retiring type. They have had definite opinions since climbing out of their cribs. I encouraged them to think. As a kid, I had people say to me, "Who asked you to think? Just do this." I resented it very much, and wanted the kids to know what they were doing and why. That sounded good, and produces intelligent adults, but children with all of those opinions are not the easiest people to tolerate. Charlie felt that he loved me, and that was all that mattered.

I was visiting a friend one day and mentioned that I was having a difficult time making a decision about Charlie. I cared about him, but I wanted to be sure I wasn't getting into another bad situation. My friend said, "If you left town, it would take him about a week to find some cute kid his age and forget you." Well, by golly if that's the case now is the time to find out, I thought, and I made a quick decision.

I leased the "cat" out, packed my family up, and left for Sacramento, California. I selected Sacramento because it was warm and far away. I hate suspense. If my relationship with Charlie was going on the rocks, I wanted to know now.

It was hard to say goodbye to him. He couldn't figure out why I thought I should go. He kissed me good-bye in Homer, he was in Anchorage to kiss me good-bye there, he wrote long letters when I got to California, and called daily. I could tell from his questions that he was worried about me, and he begged me daily to say I would marry him.

I missed him a lot, and on his birthday, the 18th of November, I asked him what he wanted most for his birthday and he said, "For you to marry me."

"You've got it." I said, and prayed that I had made a good decision for everyone concerned. He said it was the best birthday ever.

We started making plans. He was fishing in Homer, and we decided he should come take us home to Alaska. Merlie said we could be married at her place in Barstow. The '56 Mercury I was driving needed an engine overhaul before making the trip home. I made arrangements to have that done while we visited in Barstow.

Charlie wanted his friend, Alan Roehl, to be the best man. Alan was working on a seismograph boat on Cook Inlet, but it was about to close down for the season. Charlie would pick Alan up in Kenai after this last run for the season and they would go on to Anchorage and fly out. I would pick them up at the airport in Sacramento, ready for the drive to Barstow.

The day came when Charlie and Alan would arrive. I was ready to leave for the airport when the telephone rang. It was Charlie, calling from Homer. I knew when he said hello that something terrible had happened. In a sad voice he told me of an explosion on the seismograph boat that had taken Alan and his brother Bobby from us.

Charlie would have to stay for the funeral. It was a terrible shock. I was heartsick not to be there to comfort Charlie in the loss of his friend. He would come down in four days, but I would have to keep the appointment in Barstow for the engine work.

The tears rolled down my face, making wet spots on my sundress as I drove down I-5. The kids were curled up asleep as I made the turn in Bakersfield and headed out across the Mojave desert that night. It was to have been such a fun trip. I thought about Alan and how thoughtful he was bringing me the moose meat when I was having a rough time. I knew Charlie was remembering all of the fun they had together growing up in Pile Bay on Lake Iliamna. There is no easy way to lose a friend.

I had made arrangements with a neighbor to pick Charlie up from the airport, and he was waiting for us at the house when we returned. He held me tight. There was such sadness in his eyes. Losing Alan had taken its toll on his usually high spirits. Instead of the happy wedding we had planned, we went down to the court house, and were quietly married on the 28th of November.

Charlie was suffering from culture shock also. He was amazed at first at the shouting and honking of the California drivers. When I first arrived there I had spent a lot of time in tears because of their shouting, but I had toughened with time, and at this point I had no trouble returning the banter. Charlie was embarrassed. He kept scooting further down in his seat, as I shouted back at mouthy motorists. The city traffic was also upsetting to him after Homer's quiet streets.

The following week was spent loading the trailer and getting ready for the trip north. It was certainly a strange honeymoon, but everyone was in great spirits as we pulled out of Sacramento heading home to Alaska.

I was driving as we left town. There was no way Charlie was going to be involved in that Sacramento traffic. The trailer was loaded high and compact. As we went under the first overpass I said over my shoulder to Tommy who was in the back seat, "Tomtom how are things riding on the trailer?"

"Hey Mom, did you ever see a trailer with a crew cut?" It is a good thing that I am not prone to cardiac arrest. Thank goodness he was kidding.

When we were safely out on I-5 a couple of hours we stopped to gas up, and Charlie took over. He was much more legal than I, and proceeded at 55 miles an hour like it said on the signs. Immediately the siren sounded, and he got a ticket for doing five miles per hour more than he should have been when he was towing a trailer. He was upset. He had never had a ticket before, and in front of his new wife to boot.

Just outside of Grants Pass, Oregon, in a blinding rain storm he reached out to straighten the side mirror and it came off in his hand. In fifteen minutes the sirens howled again and he had ticket number two.

For a ticketless born-and-bred Alaskan, this was very disconcerting to say the least. We stayed in a motel that night in Forest Grove, Oregon. When Charlie started up onto the highway the next morning there was a high spot, and the trailer tongue hit it just enough to tear the wires lose that were connected to the trailer turn signals.

Charlie turned to me looking desperate, and said,"What am I going to do?"

"Charlie, kick this old girl up to 70, like everybody else, and head for Alaska. You go so slow they think you have a guilty conscience."

He did, and we stayed at Abbottsford, Canada, that night with no further brushes with the law. The car ran beautifully, we made good time, and the kids were really as good as five children, ranging from five to thirteen and crowded into a small area for day after day, can be.

It was 50 degrees below zero, near dusk on the sixth day of our journey. The kids were tired and to the "She's touching my arm" and "I'm being squished" stage. We were all anxious to get settled down for the night. We were fifty miles from the Alaska-Canada border, rolling along in fine shape, when a pickup came around the icy corner at about 50 mph and headed straight for us, jamming on his brakes and careening wildly.

Charlie really did a beautiful piece of driving in the next minute, saving us from a head-on collision by veering to the right into a shallow ditch. Even then, the panicky motorist hit us in the ditch and came right down the driver's side, ruining the door, hitting the trailer, breaking the hitch and spinning the trailer around. At 50 below, it shattered everything plastic. Our every belonging was scattered from hell to breakfast all over the road.

The impact had flattened the left front tire and a rock in the ditch flattened the right one. It would be dark soon, and it was obvious we weren't going anywhere very soon. I was concerned about getting the children out of the weather, although we still had the use of the car heater. A young man came along driving north and asked what he could do to help.

"Could you take my kids to the first lodge?" I asked.

"I'll be glad to," he replied.

"We will be there soon," I told the kids. "The man in the other vehicle will send a wrecker for us. Be good kids." We gathered things up off of the road and put them in the trailer as we waited for help to come. Charlie had pulled the fender up off of the tire of the offending pickup and asked the man to send help from the first garage.

When the temperature plummets far below zero the Canadian government sends a truck out to make a run before dark to help anyone who might be stranded. I thank the good Lord and the Canadian government they do this, because the panicky motorist panicked right on south without sending any help. The Canadian government truck took us to the lodge, and then started a real nightmare.

The people who ran the lodge at Alder Creek Canadian customs were absolutely impossible. They were Americans and the most difficult human beings I have ever had the misfortune of dealing with in my life. We got checked into two rooms at a cost of $100. It would be twice that today, but at that time it was the highest price we had heard of anyplace. We were all hungry and went down to the dining room for soup and sandwiches that came to $50. That finished our Canadian money, as we had expected to be in Anchorage that night and get some money from my account in Anchorage the next day. Things didn't look good, and then they got worse.

The next morning, Charlie rented the hotel pickup, with driver. They brought what was left of our trailer and belongings back to the lodge. When they returned, the nightmare gained momentum. Our belongings must be unloaded *now* but we couldn't rent a garage stall or put them anywhere on their property. The young Canadian who was driving the truck saved the day by offering, "I'm taking care of a guy's place.

You can put them there for a week, till he gets back." We took him up on his offer.

More problems: The wrecker owner from a garage 250 miles back down the road had picked up our car and brought it to the lodge, but wouldn't unhook the car until he was paid his fee of $300 in Canadian money.

"Could I give you a check?" I asked.

"Well. That will be fine if the bank will okay the check," he agreed.

I called the bank in Anchorage. They guaranteed the check. He changed his mind after I had paid the $8 for the phone call, and decided not to accept the check anyway. He would take the car to Scotty Creek on the American side, and let his nephew give him the $300. The nephew would fix our car and accept our check, holding it until Charlie returned with cash when he picked up our other things.

We breathed a sigh of relief too soon. How would the kids and I get to Scotty Creek? There was no car rental, no taxi, no bus. I walked up the stairs, lay down on the bed and dissolved into tears. A little Canadian girl doing the rooms came in, and said sympathetically, "What is the matter, dearie?"

She shook her head sympathetically as I wailed out my woes. After finishing vacuuming the hallway she came back and sat down on the bed beside me where I still lay sobbing away. I am not usually such a wimp.

"My boyfriend is coming to take me for a ride this afternoon, and I am sure he won't mind taking you to Scotty Creek."

If it hadn't been for the Canadian people working at the lodge we might be sitting up there yet. Wonderful people!

The bunch at Scotty Creek worked far into the night to put the new tires on the Merc, and cut and weld on the fenders. Early the next morning we were on the road, going through US customs as soon as they opened. When we crossed the border we all cheered. Alaska looked so very good. That Merc was a wonderful car. Even after the beating it took, it hummed along. We began to think in terms of what we would do when we got to Homer, but... the nightmare was not finished.

Just out of Tok Junction a wheel bearing went out. Charlie hitched a ride into Tok. The kids and I waited in the car with the motor running and heater going full blast to combat the still 50 degrees below zero outside. I said a silent prayer that

Charlie would make it back before we ran out of gas. Luckily, he managed to find the part. A kind person drove him back, and helped to install it. Once again we were on the road.

We drove straight through from Tok to Homer and home sweet home. Whenever anyone says "Alcan" it gives me the whips and the jingles. Charlie did a quick turnaround to retrieve our things. He took fresh king crab to the nice kids who had helped us at the lodge and to the bunch at Scotty Creek.

His second trip was accomplished without mishap. We were home! Ready to start our life together. We were broke, it was late fall, the car was a mess on the outside, Christmas time was coming, but what is life without a few challenges?

Chapter 23

Home Sweet Homer

Our homecoming in late November was to the little uninsulated homesite cabin on the lake where the kids and I had stayed when I first left Lloyd. It was up on piling, and winter breezes played unchecked beneath it. Keeping it warm was impossible. We would have to find a place in town soon.

I heard the Adventists wanted to move their church to another lot and the person in charge was Elder Zumwalt. I remembered him from Walla Walla days. He and his family used to come for dinner and to visit my aunt and uncle. I went to see him.

"If we move the church for you, could we have the parsonage as payment?" I asked after we visited a bit.

"Sounds like a fair deal to me," he said, pleased to have that worry off of his mind. I was pleased too.

Charlie borrowed his dad's "cat" and made it happen.

It was a short move, and soon we were snug in our little house in town. My old house had burned, and this one now sat in its place. I sold the cabin from the homesite for money to get us settled. Charlie picked up odd jobs and kept us eating. We were on a tight budget, but no one went hungry. When you are in those tight spots it makes your brain work harder.

It may sound crazy, but that was a happy winter. Monopoly and Chinese checkers with Charlie and the kids, and reading books made the time fly by. There is a lot to be said for the pre-television days. We took time for each other. Charlie was good to me and to my kids. He never let me wonder if I was loved. Who could ask for more?

Charlie's mom wasn't happy about our marriage. I think she liked me personally, but I was twelve years older than he and had five kids. Being a mother, I understood her feelings. I chose to ignore the matter as there was nothing I could do about it.

One thing I had in common with my father-in-law, Carl, was being an early morning person. By 5:30 a.m. he liked to be up doing something constructive. When he was ready for a coffee break around 7 a.m., I would get a cup of peppermint tea, and one of us would call the other on the phone. He was a mechanical genius and I enjoyed hearing about his shop projects. His wonderful sense of humor started my day off with a smile.

When Charlie's and my son David was born in 1963, Charlie was ecstatic. He looked so much like his dad I felt like a copy machine. My older kids thought they had acquired a new doll and loved him immensely. Charlie's teen-age sisters, Ruby and Pauline, were running the Family Cafe across the street. They loved to cuddle David whenever they got a chance.

During the labor hours before David's arrival, Charlie held my hand. I awoke to flowers at my bedside. It was a first, and I loved it. In the midst of my labor, Charlie called his dad and said in a worried voice, "Dad, she's hurting, and I don't know what to do to help."

Dad, of course, assured him that us girls had been taking care of this little project for years. I would do just fine. But it was so nice to have him care.

Charlie worked at the cannery in the herring fishing season. When that was over, he worked some at Hollace's service station across the street. I picked up some waitress work but we were leading a hand-to-mouth existence. It was time to do some concrete planning for our future.

That fall, son Tommy came in the house full of enthusiasm and said, "Mom, Homie Terrill (next-door neighbor's son) just got back from fishing at Bristol Bay. I want to go there next year. He made pretty good money."

I thought about that for a moment. He was only thirteen years old. Realizing that with Tom it would be tough getting him to listen to anything that sounded like no, I did the evasive mother tactic.

"Hmmm. Well it is a long time till spring, and we can talk about that later. Would you get me a bucket of coal, honey"?

I filed it mentally under "a Tommy bright idea, not too important," and assumed he would soon forget. Wrong! I was sitting with the Sears catalogue in early October, making out an order for the kids' winter clothes. Tommy came and hung over my shoulder to see what I was doing.

"Mom, when you order my long john's, be sure and get them a size bigger."

"Why honey?" I asked.

"Then I'll be able to wear them out at Bristol Bay next summer. Homie says it gets pretty cold on those night picks."

Ooops, what do we have here? This idea is still floating around? Well really, what harm can come of getting his long johns a little big? So I said "Mmmhmm," and ordered the long johns in a size 14.

The first serious discussion came in January.

"Mom, could you get the forms for my fishing license for Bristol Bay? I don't want any last minute hang-ups."

He looked at me for a minute waiting for an answer, I was on the spot. This had to be settled.

"And would you write to the people Homie worked for so I can be sure and have a spot to fish?"

"Sit down, son." I poured myself a cup of tea and took a deep breath. This wouldn't be easy, but it was time.

"Tommy, you are only thirteen years old. It would be wrong for me to let you go out where there is hardly any communication. Where I wouldn't know if you were being fed. It would be gross negligence on my part to agree to such a thing."

Now if you think, with his Scottish-Welsh record for determination, that was the end of the story you are wrong.

"Mom, I need to make money and I do not want to become a full-grown paper boy."

He had a point there. Finally I sighed and said, "Tommy, I will talk to Homie's mother and get the details."

That only got me off of the hook for a couple of days. Sensing my reluctance, Tommy had gotten his fishing license himself, paying for it with money from his paper route. Now I had to do something.

"Okay Tom, I'll make you a deal. I found out a man's name and address who has people fish for him at Bristol Bay. I will write him. If he'll take us, we will all go, and if he won't, no more discussion on the matter. Deal?"

Tomtom grinned and hugged me.

"Okay, it's a deal. You'll see, Mom, it will be just fine."

His exuberance made me feel a little guilty, as I didn't think anyone in their right mind would take a woman with a half dozen kids ranging from eighteen months to fifteen years. Especially to that far off remote area of Bristol Bay.

Charlie gave the idea his reluctant blessing. He had already made arrangements to commercial fish on the Inlet so would not be going with us if we were approved. We decided that if anything came of this it could be advantageous to have a double shot at winter groceries with two incomes.

The outcome of that decision is another whole story. It is called *This Is Coffee Point... Go Ahead*. It changed the path of all of our lives and brought me many years of adventure and happiness.

Epilogue

The busy years have flown by. The children are all grown and have lives of their own. Occasionally, I have the pleasure of having some of my grandchildren with me for a visit. Since the Bristol Bay years I tried retiring but that is a difficult thing to do. There are so many interesting projects to do. I have gotten involved in building and renting. I have wonderful renters who have become part of my life.

In spite of the rebellious beginnings, I love the State of Alaska and hope to see more of it in the next few years. I took a trip to Nome a few years ago and it was like going back in time to the years before we had a road in Homer. An elderly gentleman stopped me on the street and wanted to know where I had come from and what I was doing there. I spent a good deal of time in their library and was fascinated to find that Hoagy Carmichael had played piano in the bars there as a nine-year-old. He was accompanied by his father, who also was a musician. Jimmy Doolittle, of World War II fame, also spent time in Nome in his early years.

My friend, Reenie, and I took a trip to the Pribilofs and enjoyed every minute of our brief visit. We were a little alarmed when we arrived and found the hotel door locked. After thinking a minute, I just asked one of the youngsters who were riding their bikes around and eyeing us curiously, if they would please get the person with the key. No problem.

I have had the pleasure of visiting all of the towns along the southeastern shores of our fair state. In Sitka we played tourist, walking among the ancient totem poles that were in the process of being restored and savoring the interesting information in their museum.

I lived in Ketchikan briefly and there, again, were the totem poles, remnants of yesteryear. About the time you have had all of the rain you can stand the sun comes out, shining on the rugged mountains and making the water glisten. You forgive all and stand in awe of its beauty.

Juneau clings tenaciously to the abrupt mountainside, bustling with political activity and steeped in history. At night the lights shining out across Gastinau Channels are simply beautiful.

Petersburg's seafood canneries that go back to Alaska's early days, its waterways among the islands and the clean well-painted village all make such a beautiful picture.

I spent several years in Kodiak when it was bustling with the activities connected with the seafood industry in the wake of the 1964 earthquake. In the early days of the crab fishing, fortunes were made by the boat owners who harvested the king crab. Those crab often measured six feet across. Baranof's castle, from whence he first governed the Russian colony, has been made into a museum. On the waterfront in front of the castle is the Standard Oil office, but buried beneath it are the remains of the trading post building. Early hunters brought their boats beneath the building to display and unload their furs through trapdoors in the floor. On the hill stands the Russian Orthodox church, where villagers rang the bell until blood ran from their hands in order that every local person could find their way to safety, through the volcanic ash from the eruption of Mount Katmai in 1909. That is a whole story in itself.

Back here in Southcentral Alaska there is Anchorage that grew from the barracks of a military post to be our largest city, with all of the conveniences of our modern-day world, including international flights. On the other hand we all look forward to the Fur Rendezvous with its dog sled races, which brings mushers and dogs flying in from remote villages all over the state to compete.

The villages along the shores of Cook Inlet are rich in history. Not only Russian history but of the Dena'ina and other tribes of original inhabitants. There have been ancient oil-burning stone lamps found in the area that date back thousands of years.

Last, but not least, there is Homer. That place I darn well was not going to stay. It is built on what, in some ancient time, was a slide area. We know it was the home of ancient tribes as there are middens and other evidence at various places around Kachemak Bay. It has a wealth of coal beneath its grassy slopes that was mined commercially in the late 1800s. In fact Homer got its name from one of the managers, Homer Pennock. On the sandy beaches of the Homer Spit, during the gold rush days, at times there were several hundred people trying to get up Hope, to what they hoped was another big strike. They would build rafts and small boats or they would walk. The latter was probably the safest idea, unless they were experienced boat builders. Across the bay are the glaciers and, high up, bits of the Harding Ice Field. Across Cook Inlet you can see Mounts Augustine, Iliamna and Redoubt periodically sending up their little spirals of smoke. Now and then they get more boisterous and put on a big volcanic show, shooting boulders 30,000 feet into the air.

This has been a love story about me and Alaska. I haven't been to Point Barrow or Dutch Harbor yet. I would love to do that. Maybe next year.

The End

Order Form

Please send the following books:

___ copies of *If You've Got It To Do* @ $15.95

___ copies of *This is Coffee Point...Go Ahead* @ $15.95.

I have enclosed a check for $_____, including postage and handling of $2.00 for the first book and $.50 for each additional book.

Your Name_____

Address _____

City/State/Zip _____

MAIL THIS FORM WITH PAYMENT TO

Wizard Works
P.O. Box 1125   or   **Wilma Williams**
Homer, AK 99603   **P.O. Box 1232**
                       Homer, AK 99603

Order Form

Please send the following books:

___ copies of *If You've Got It To Do* @ $15.95

___ copies of *This is Coffee Point...Go Ahead* @ $15.95.

I have enclosed a check for $_____, including postage and handling of $2.00 for the first book and $.50 for each additional book.

Your Name_____

Address _____

City/State/Zip _____

MAIL THIS FORM WITH PAYMENT TO

Wizard Works   **Wilma Williams**
P.O. Box 1125   or   **P.O. Box 1232**
Homer, AK 99603   **Homer, AK 99603**